CAMBRIDGE
UNIVERSITY PRESS

CAMBRIDGE ENGLISH
Language Assessment
Part of the University of Cambridge

T0343893

Cambridge English

OFFICIAL
PREPARATION MATERIAL

EXAM BOOSTER WITH ANSWER KEY

FOR FIRST AND FIRST FOR SCHOOLS

Self-study edition

Helen Chilton, Sheila Dignen, Mark Fountain and Frances Treloar

Cambridge University Press
www.cambridge.org/elt

Cambridge Assessment English
www.cambridgeenglish.org

Information on this title: www.cambridge.org/9781108553933

First published 2017

20 19 18 17 16 15 14

Printed in Great Britain by Ashford Colour Ltd.

Legal deposit: M-30600-2017

A catalogue record for this publication is available from the British Library

ISBN 978-1-108-55393-3

Additional resources for this publication at www.cambridge.org/firstbooster

Cambridge University Press has no responsibility for the persistence or accuracy of URLs for external or third-party internet websites referred to in this publication, and does not guarantee that any content on such websites is, or will remain, accurate or appropriate. Information regarding prices, travel timetables, and other factual information given in this work is correct at the time of first printing but Cambridge University Press does not guarantee the accuracy of such information thereafter.

CONTENTS

MAP OF THE BOOK

Paper 1: Reading and Use of English 1 hour 15 minutes	Worksheet 1	Worksheet 2	Worksheet 3
Part 1 p12 4-option multiple-choice cloze 8 questions / 8 marks	**Hobbies and leisure** Adjectives + preposition Hobbies and leisure vocabulary	**Travel and holidays** Prepositions of location and movement Commonly confused words	**Sport** Verb + noun collocations *-ing* and *to* + infinitive
Part 2 p18 Open cloze 8 questions / 8 marks	**Health and fitness** Articles, quantifiers and determiners Relative clauses and relative pronouns	**Education and study** Linking expressions Verb + noun collocations	**Family and friends** Personal, possessive and reflexive pronouns Phrasal verbs
Part 3 p24 Word formation 8 questions / 8 marks	**Science and technology** Word formation: adjective suffixes Word families	**Food and drink** Word formation: noun suffixes Spelling	**The natural world** Word formation: negative prefixes Spelling
Part 4 p30 Key word transformation 6 questions / 12 marks	**Travel and holidays** Present forms Comparison	**Daily life** Reported speech Reported questions	**Weather** Phrasal verbs Conditionals with *if* and *unless*
Part 5 p36 4-option multiple choice 6 questions / 12 marks	**Science and technology** Technology vocabulary	**House and home** Future forms	**Work** *wish*, *hope* and *if only*
Part 6 p42 Gapped text 6 questions / 12 marks	**The natural world** Modals: obligation, permission and prohibition	**Health and fitness** Health and fitness vocabulary Modals: obligation, permission and prohibition	**Education and study** Education and study vocabulary Modals: possibility and certainty
Part 7 p48 Multiple matching 10 questions / 10 marks	**Cultures and customs** The passive	**Entertainment and media** *have / get something done*	**The environment** The passive with reporting verbs
Paper 2: Writing 1 hour 20 minutes	**Worksheet 1**	**Worksheet 2**	**Worksheet 3**
Part 1 p54 Writing an essay 1 question / 20 marks	**Hobbies and leisure** Expressing opinions Linking words: cohesion	**Health and fitness** Comparing and contrasting opinions Linking words: contrast	**The environment** Environmental issues vocabulary Writing concluding paragraphs

	Worksheet 1	**Worksheet 2**	**Worksheet 3**
Part 2 p60 Writing an article, a letter or email, a review, a report or a story 1 question from a choice of 4 20 marks	**Travel and holidays** Travel and holidays vocabulary Linking words: narration	**Cultures and customs** Giving advice and making suggestions Informal language	**Education and work** Education vocabulary Relative clauses and relative pronouns
	Worksheet 4	**Worksheet 5**	**Worksheet 6**
	Shopping and fashion Adjectives: opinions Making recommendations	**Places and buildings** Making suggestions and recommendations for change Punctuation	**Family and friends** Narrative tenses Descriptive adverbs

Paper 3: Listening 40 minutes	**Worksheet 1**	**Worksheet 2**	**Worksheet 3**
Part 1 p72 3-option multiple choice 8 questions / 8 marks	**Education and study** *Yes / no* questions and short answers Adjectives: feelings and emotions	**Hobbies and leisure** Adjectives ending *-ing* and *-ed* Question tags and question words	**Health and fitness** Agreeing / disagreeing (*So do I*, *Neither have I* etc.) Health and fitness vocabulary
Part 2 p78 Sentence completion 10 questions / 10 marks	**Food and drink** Parts of speech Phrasal verbs	**Work** Work vocabulary Linking words	**The natural world** Natural world vocabulary Present perfect simple and present perfect continuous
Part 3 p84 Multiple matching 5 questions / 5 marks	**Shopping and fashion** Shopping and fashion vocabulary Past forms	**Places and buildings** Buildings vocabulary *used to* and *be / get used to*	**Travel and holidays** Adjectives: feelings and emotions Air travel vocabulary
Part 4 p90 3-option multiple choice 7 questions / 7 marks	**Cultures and customs** Cultures and customs vocabulary Descriptive adverbs	**The environment** Environment vocabulary Phrasal verbs	**Sport** Sport vocabulary *too* and *enough*

Paper 4: Speaking 14 minutes	**Worksheet 1**	**Worksheet 2**	**Worksheet 3**
Part 1 p96 Examiner interviews candidates / 2 minutes	**Family and friends** *be like*, *look like*, *like*, and *alike* Asking for clarification and repetition	**Hobbies and leisure** Giving reasons Linking words: cause and effect	**Education and work** Giving yourself time to think Expressing plans and hopes for the future
Part 2 p102 Comparing two photographs / 4 minutes	**Shopping** Comparing photographs Modals: speculation and deduction	**Hobbies and leisure** Discourse markers Dealing with difficulties when speaking	**Travel and holidays** Comparing photographs Describing photographs with *look*, *seem* and *appear*
Parts 3 and 4 p108 Discussion and decision-making task / Further discussion / 8 minutes	**Health and fitness** Making suggestions Asking for other people's opinions	**Family and friends** Giving and clarifying opinions Making concluding statements and decisions	**Education and study** Agreeing and disagreeing Giving balanced opinions

Think about it p114

Answer key p122

HOW TO USE THE EXAM BOOSTER

Welcome to the Cambridge English BOOSTER

What is the Exam Booster?

The Exam Booster provides focused exam practice of all parts of the *Cambridge English: First (FCE)* and *Cambridge English: First (FCE) for Schools* exam. Prepare for the exam, ensuring you gain the confidence, skills and knowledge you need for exam day.

How can I use it?

- Pick and choose the areas you want to practise at any time
- Use alongside a coursebook or on its own
- Download the audio to your computer or device – Go to www.cambridge.org/firstbooster

How is it structured?

The Exam Booster contains 16 sections which follow the order of the exam: Reading and Use of English Parts 1–7, Writing Parts 1–2, Listening Parts 1–4 and finally Speaking Parts 1–4.

Check exam paper, exam part and worksheet number at the top of each section.

Cover a variety of topics from the exam. Topics are suitable for both *Cambridge English: First* and *Cambridge English: First for Schools* preparation.

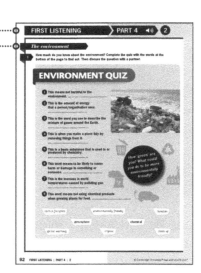

Go to www.cambridge.org/firstbooster to download the audio to your computer or device.

Find exam tasks easily. There are three worksheets for each exam part.

Exam facts offer clear, concise information about the exercise type and number of questions.

What other features are there?

Practise vocabulary, grammar or functional language tested in the exam using the additional tasks on the worksheet.

Exam tips provide practical strategies and advice on how to approach the task.

Avoid the most typical mistakes that candidates make with *Get it right!* Identify and correct common errors made by real *Cambridge English: First* and *Cambridge English: First for Schools* exam candidates.

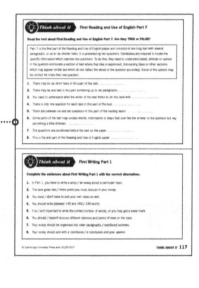

Use *Think about it* sections to check you understand what you need to do for each part of the exam – great either before or after attempting an exercise.

Access a complete Answer key with sample answers for the writing tasks and Audioscript.

Paper 1: Reading and Use of English   1 hour 15 mins

Reading and Use of English

Part	Number of questions	Number of marks	Task type	Task format
1	8	8	Multiple-choice cloze	A text in which there are eight missing words or phrases. Candidates have to choose the correct option (A, B, C or D) to fill each gap.
2	8	8	Open cloze	A text in which there are eight missing words. Candidates have to think of the correct word to fill each gap.
3	8	8	Word formation	A text in which there are eight gaps. Candidates have to change a prompt word to form the correct missing word that fills each gap.
4	6	12	Key word transformation	Six pairs of sentences. Candidates have to complete the second sentence in each pair, using a given key word, so that it has the same meaning as the first sentence.
5	6	12	Multiple choice	A text with six multiple-choice questions. Candidates have to decide which option (A, B, C or D) is the correct answer to each question.
6	6	12	Gapped text	A text in which there are six gaps and a list of sentences. Candidates have to choose the correct sentence to fill each gap.
7	10	10	Multiple matching	A long text or several short texts and ten statements. For each statement, candidates have to decide which part of the text contains the information mentioned.
Total	52	70		

Paper 2: Writing 1 hour 20 mins

Writing

Part	Number of questions	Number of marks	Task type	Task format
1	1	20	An essay	Candidates are given an essay title and two ideas. They must write an essay of 140–190 words, using the points given and adding an idea of their own.
2	1 from a choice of 4	20	An article, a letter/email, a review, a report or a story	Candidates write 140–190 words, answering the question of their choosing in the way specified.
Total	2	40		

Paper 3: Listening 🔊

About 40 mins

Part	Number of questions	Number of marks	Task type	Task format
1	8	8	Multiple choice	Eight short monologues or conversations. Candidates have to decide which option (A, B or C) is the answer to a question about each recording.
2	10	10	Sentence completion	A monologue lasting 3–4 minutes. Candidates have to complete ten sentences with information from the recording.
3	5	5	Multiple matching	Five short related monologues. Candidates have to choose which statement from a list of eight best matches what each speaker says.
4	7	7	Multiple choice	An interview or discussion between two speakers of 3–4 minutes. Candidates have to decide which option (A, B or C) answers each of the eight questions.
Total	30	30		

Paper 4: Speaking

About 14 mins

Part	Timing	Interaction	Task type	Task format
1	2 minutes	Examiner ↓ Candidate	Interview	The examiner asks the candidates questions about themselves. They may be asked to talk about past experiences, present circumstances and future plans.
2	4 minutes	Candidate long turn	Long turn	Each candidate has to talk about and compare a pair of colour photographs for one minute without interruption. They also have to answer a short question about the other candidate's photographs.
3	4 minutes	Candidate ↕ Candidate	Collaborative task	The examiner gives the candidates a question and some written prompts. The candidates discuss these together for two minutes. The examiner will then ask them to make a decision together about the topic they have been discussing.
4	4 minutes	Candidate ↕ Candidate	Discussion	Further discussion between the candidates, guided by questions from the examiner, about the same topic as the task in Part 3.
	Total	60 marks		

Cambridge English

The Cambridge English Scale explained

A guide to converting *Cambridge English: First* and *First for Schools* practice test scores to Cambridge English Scale scores

Cambridge English: First and *First for Schools* are now reporting results on the Cambridge English Scale. For these exams, candidates receive an individual score for each of the four skills – reading, writing, listening, speaking – and Use of English. In the live exams, each of the skills and Use of English are equally weighted, and a candidate's overall score is calculated by adding all of the individual scores together and dividing by five (and then rounding to the nearest whole number). A candidate's grade and CEFR level are based on their performance across the whole test, and there is no requirement to achieve a minimum score in each paper.

The following tables can be used as guidance to help you convert practice test scores to Cambridge English Scale scores.

Please note that these only apply when using official Cambridge English practice tests.

The conversion tables are only intended as a guide for your readiness to take the exam. Your scores may not always reflect the results you may achieve in the live exam. They should not be used to try to predict precise scores in the live exam, but can be a useful diagnostic tool, indicating areas of relative strength and weakness.

The scores needed on any given test to achieve the scores on the Cambridge English Scale shown in the tables below will vary due to a number of factors, so scores close to CEFR boundaries need to be reviewed carefully. We recommend that this is approximately three Cambridge English Scale score points above and below the score needed to achieve the level, e.g. 157–163 for Level B2. Students who achieve only slightly higher than the Cambridge English Scale score for a given level on a practice test may not achieve that level in the live exam, and we recommend that they continue working to improve so that they reach the desired level.

CAMBRIDGE ENGLISH
Language Assessment
Part of the University of Cambridge

Cambridge English
First

Cambridge English
First
for Schools

Reading

The Reading section consists of Parts 1, 5, 6 and 7 of the Reading and Use of English paper. Correct answers in Parts 1 and 7 are worth 1 mark each. Correct answers in Parts 5 and 6 are worth 2 marks each. There are 42 possible marks in the Reading section.

Practice test score	Cambridge English Scale score	CEFR Level
37	180	Level C1
24	160	Level B2
16	140	Level B1
10	122*	-

*minimum score reported for *First*

Use of English

The Use of English section consists of Parts 2, 3 and 4 of the Reading and Use of English paper. Correct answers in Parts 2 and 3 are worth 1 mark each. In Part 4, answers which are partly correct receive 1 mark and answers which are completely correct receive 2 marks. There are 28 possible marks in the Use of English section.

Practice test score	Cambridge English Scale score	CEFR Level
24	180	Level C1
18	160	Level B2
11	140	Level B1
7	122*	-

*minimum score reported for *First*

Writing

Candidates' answers in the Writing paper are marked by trained examiners who are certificated to mark at the level. Answers are marked using assessment scales which are linked to the Common European Framework of Reference. 0-5 marks are given for each of the following criteria: Content; Communicative Achievement; Organisation; and Language. Whole marks only are awarded; there are no half marks given. Marks for each of the criteria are combined to give 20 possible marks for each question. There are 40 possible marks for the whole paper.

Practice test score	Cambridge English Scale score	CEFR Level
34	180	Level C1
24	160	Level B2
16	140	Level B1
10	122*	-

*minimum score reported for *First*

Listening

Correct answers in the Listening paper are worth 1 mark each. There are 30 possible marks in the Listening paper.

Practice test score	Cambridge English Scale score	CEFR Level
27	180	Level C1
18	160	Level B2
12	140	Level B1
8	122*	-

*minimum score reported for *First*

Speaking

Candidates take the test in pairs, but are assessed on their individual performance by trained examiners certificated to examine at the level. Candidate speaking performances are assessed using scales which are linked to the Common European Framework of Reference. The assessor gives 0-5 marks for each of the following criteria: Grammar and Vocabulary; Discourse Management; Pronunciation; and Interactive Communication. Marks for each of these criteria are doubled. The interlocutor gives a mark of 0-5 for Global Achievement. This mark is then multiplied by four. Examiners may award half marks. Marks for all criteria are then combined, meaning there are 60 marks available in the Speaking test.

Practice test score	Cambridge English Scale score	CEFR Level
54	180	Level C1
36	160	Level B2
24	140	Level B1
14	122*	-

*minimum score reported for *First*

Hobbies and leisure

1a **Complete the sentences with the correct word from the box.**

about	at	by	in	into	on	to	with

1. I'm not very keen .... science fiction films, but the rest of my family loves them.
2. I'm interested .... taking up scuba diving, but it's an expensive hobby.
3. My father has always been fascinated .... architecture and loves visiting old castles.
4. I used to prefer rock and folk music, but I've really got .... jazz recently.
5. John is very excited .... starting tennis lessons next week.
6. Maria is quite pleased .... her daughter's progress in her ballet class.
7. Some people can become addicted .... playing computer games.
8. Antonia is brilliant .... cooking; I wish I could do it as well as her!

1b **Complete the sentences with the correct preposition and your own ideas.**

1. I'm very keen ....
2. My best friend is brilliant ....
3. I'm really excited ....
4. Many people are addicted ....
5. Lately, I've really got ....

2 **Choose the correct alternative to complete the sentences.**

1. The *viewers / spectators* in the stadium cheered for their team.
2. Jacob decided to take *place / part* in a cooking competition.
3. Rachel *took / set* up painting because she wanted to make better use of her free time.
4. I really enjoyed the *demonstration / exhibition* of eighteenth-century art at the city gallery.
5. My favourite singer is *giving / running* a concert in my home town and I hope to see her.
6. I go to the cinema regularly and like to see *moving / thrilling* films that are very emotional.
7. Elena enjoys reading detective stories with complicated but interesting *schemes / plots*.
8. He is a very *sociable / sensible* person who loves meeting new people in his free time.

3

For questions 1–8, read the text below and decide which answer (A, B, C or D) best fits each gap. There is an example at the beginning (0).

Example:

0 **A** taste   **B** appeal   **C** interest   **D** attraction

Example answer: *B*

The joy of photography

Photography is a hobby with wide **(0)** .... And I don't mean taking photos on your mobile phone, though it cannot be **(1)** .... that such pictures can be surprisingly good these days. Serious photography means taking the **(2)** .... to do some research, exploring the technical **(3)** .... of the subject and investing in what might be quite expensive equipment. So why take up photography? Firstly, it allows you to **(4)** .... special moments that you want to remember forever. In addition, it **(5)** .... your imagination because you are always in search of ideas for original and out of the ordinary photos.

However, a lot of practice is required before you **(6)** .... to take really good pictures on a regular basis. When you finally do it, it will be a **(7)** .... of great satisfaction for you. Photography can also transform the way you look at the world. You start to see details that in the past you used to miss **(8)** .... All in all, it's a highly absorbing hobby.

1 **A** rejected	**B** contradicted	**C** denied	**D** refused
2 **A** trouble	**B** care	**C** effort	**D** concern
3 **A** characteristics	**B** forms	**C** qualities	**D** aspects
4 **A** seize	**B** capture	**C** grab	**D** catch
5 **A** motivates	**B** renews	**C** stimulates	**D** reacts
6 **A** manage	**B** succeed	**C** achieve	**D** reach
7 **A** reason	**B** cause	**C** source	**D** means
8 **A** utterly	**B** completely	**C** fully	**D** absolutely

 Exam facts

- In this part, you read a text with eight gaps in it.
- You have to choose the correct word (A, B, C or D) for each gap.

Travel and holidays

1 ▶ **Complete the sentences with the correct word from the box.**

along	among	around	back	beneath	beyond	through	within

1. Luke saw his friends .... the crowd of tourists outside the castle.
2. I went for a tour .... the city and was impressed by how beautiful it was.
3. In Rome there are kilometres of tunnels .... the city.
4. It was getting late so we decided to head .... to the campsite.
5. It was really relaxing taking a walk .... the river.
6. In the distance, ... the mountain range, there is a huge lake.
7. Our guide led us .... the caves and showed us their interesting features.
8. Many important events have happened .... the walls of this palace.

2 ▶ **Choose the alternative for each sentence which is NOT correct.**

1. We went on a *travel / trip / journey* to the jungle.
2. I enjoyed the beautiful *view / scenery / outlook* from the top of the hill.
3. The family *boarded / got on / embarked* the bus and it left almost immediately.
4. Giorgio packed his two *bags / luggage / suitcases* and took the early train.
5. The train *fare / fee / ticket* was much more expensive than Anna expected.
6. On the way to Scotland we sat in the front *coach / carriage / cabin* of the train.
7. A river *voyage / trip / cruise* is the best way to go sightseeing.
8. We decided to take a *charter / programmed / scheduled* flight to Spain.

3 ▶ **In pairs, ask and answer the following questions.**

1. Where do you usually go on holiday?
2. Do you usually go to places where there are lots of tourists, or do you go to less well-known places?
3. What do you think are the advantages and disadvantages of exploring less well-known places when travelling?

☑ Exam task

4 For questions 1–8, read the text below and decide which answer (A, B, C or D) best fits each gap. There is an example at the beginning (0).

Example:

0 **A** represent   **B** indicate   **C** refer   **D** mention

Example answer: *C*

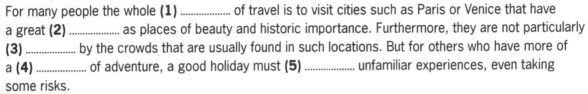

Off the beaten track

The expression 'getting off the beaten track' is used to **(0)** .... to the experience of avoiding famous tourist attractions and choosing instead to explore less well-known places when travelling.
For many people the whole **(1)** .... of travel is to visit cities such as Paris or Venice that have a great **(2)** .... as places of beauty and historic importance. Furthermore, they are not particularly **(3)** .... by the crowds that are usually found in such locations. But for others who have more of a **(4)** .... of adventure, a good holiday must **(5)** .... unfamiliar experiences, even taking some risks.

Travelling off the beaten track may be done by some students who don't **(6)** .... to a rigid plan, but make decisions about what to do depending on how they feel. Other travellers prefer to spend money on guided tours to unusual locations. Such tours are designed to **(7)** .... their particular needs, and all the arrangements are made for them. However people choose to get off the beaten track, the hope is always the same: to have a special, often unique **(8)** .... of a different culture.

1	**A** worth	**B** point	**C** aim	**D** profit
2	**A** favour	**B** approval	**C** reputation	**D** opinion
3	**A** bothered	**B** interrupted	**C** offended	**D** disturbed
4	**A** feeling	**B** impression	**C** mood	**D** sense
5	**A** possess	**B** consist	**C** involve	**D** concern
6	**A** fix	**B** stick	**C** fasten	**D** attach
7	**A** please	**B** fit	**C** agree	**D** meet
8	**A** experience	**B** understanding	**C** awareness	**D** knowledge

☑ Exam tips

- Read through the whole text first.
- Look at the words before and after each gap.
- Try each word (A, B, C and D) in the gap and decide which is correct. If you are not sure, choose the word that you think best fits the gap.

Sport

1 **Choose the correct verb to complete the sentences.**

1. I *play / practise / go* jogging every morning before work.
2. I *go / take / make* plenty of exercise every week because I walk to work!
3. Most experts say that *keeping / going / making* fit is very important if you sit at a desk all day.
4. Tony *plays / practises / makes* tennis at a local club when he has some free time.
5. Clara *hit / beat / shot* the ball really hard and it went into the net.
6. The class *make / do / play* gymnastics once a week in the new gym.
7. The school football team *beat / won / succeeded* every team they played this term.
8. I did a course to *develop / expand / progress* my tennis skills.

2a **Complete the sentences with the correct form of the verb in brackets, *-ing* or *to* + infinitive.**

1. Elena can't stand .... (play) football; she prefers athletics.
2. I regretted .... (do) the extra training session because I felt so tired afterwards.
3. Lucas is planning .... (take up) skiing next year.
4. Nicole really enjoys .... (go) for long runs in the hills near her home.
5. The squash player managed .... (win) the final game despite being exhausted.
6. Leo refused .... (join) his local gym even though his friends were all members.
7. My mother is considering .... (enter) a golf tournament next month.
8. We knew we were unlikely .... (lose) against a very weak and inexperienced team.

2b **Complete the sentences with your own ideas.**

1. I can't stand ....
2. I'm considering ....
3. My friends and I really enjoy ....
4. The weather is likely ....
5. My family's planning ....

☑ *Exam task*

For questions 1–8, read the text below and decide which answer (A, B, C or D) best fits each gap. There is an example at the beginning (0).

Example:

0   A complete   **B** finish   **C** fulfil   **D** succeed

Example answer: *C*

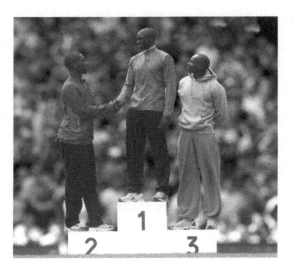

Coming second: pleasure or pain?

Every ambitious athlete hopes to **(0)** .... their dream of winning a gold medal at the Olympics. However, not everyone can win, and often talented athletes must accept second place. A team of psychologists recently **(1)** .... some research on the emotional responses of those finishing second. For certain individuals, a silver medal may **(2)** .... their expectations and so naturally they will be delighted. They may also enjoy surprising experts and journalists who believed they had absolutely no **(3)** .... of achieving anything.

In **(4)** ...., the athlete who everyone assumed would win with ease, but then suffers a **(5)** .... defeat, may not celebrate their silver medal. This reaction differs sharply from the athlete who comes second but finished a long way behind the winner. There is a **(6)** .... in the research that shows such a person will feel significantly happier.

To a certain **(7)** ...., these findings are not surprising. Silver medallists who were close to victory will almost certainly **(8)** .... on what might have happened if they had trained harder, or done things differently.

1	**A** controlled	**B** conducted	**C** directed	**D** guided
2	**A** exceed	**B** overtake	**C** pass	**D** overcome
3	**A** outlook	**B** view	**C** estimate	**D** prospect
4	**A** opposition	**B** contrast	**C** distinction	**D** contradiction
5	**A** thin	**B** tight	**C** narrow	**D** slight
6	**A** habit	**B** trend	**C** custom	**D** tendency
7	**A** extent	**B** amount	**C** range	**D** level
8	**A** review	**B** wonder	**C** consider	**D** reflect

◉ *Get it right!*

Look at the sentence below. Then try to correct the mistake.

When I was at primary school, I enjoyed to play basketball.

Health and fitness

1 Complete the text with the words in the box. There are two words you do not need to use.

a	all	an	both	every	few	much	that	the	those

Michael Green loved swimming from **(1)** .... early age. He took **(2)** .... opportunity that came along to spend time in his local pool. As he got older, he regularly entered local competitions, **(3)** .... of which he won. This perfect record attracted a lot of attention and he started working with a coach. **(4)** .... training sessions paid off and Michael rapidly improved his speed and strength. However, **(5)** .... believed that he would continue to work so hard, especially when he had so **(6)** .... schoolwork to do. But winning **(7)** .... national championship was his dream, and **(8)** .... was what motivated him. However, Michael went on to achieve even more than this, becoming the world champion before his eighteenth birthday.

☑ Exam task

2 For questions 1–8, read the text below and think of the word which best fits each gap. Use only one word in each gap. There is an example at the beginning (0).

Example: (0) *NO*

Running a marathon

So you want to run a marathon? There is **(0)** .... doubt that running 42 kilometres is a great achievement. Many training plans involve running four times a week for at **(1)** .... three months, and sometimes longer. Experts strongly recommend that you should **(2)** .... used to running long distances gradually. If you don't, it can increase the chances **(3)** .... picking up an injury. It **(4)** .... generally thought that runners should initially go on fairly relaxed training runs. The pace should be gentle enough to allow you **(5)** .... have a conversation with someone running alongside you.

Don't make the mistake of eating too little before the race, or you will rapidly run **(6)** .... of energy. But **(7)** .... should you eat a large meal. It goes without saying that choosing the right footwear is also essential. **(8)** .... you do, avoid clothes made of cotton and go for artificial materials, or even some types of wool such as merino. Choose clothing that will be comfortable.

Read the sentences. Choose the correct word for each space, a, b or c.

1. The diet .... I'm on is quite boring, to be honest.

   a who   **b** what   **c** which

2. My fitness trainer is someone .... everyone likes and trusts.

   a which   **b** who   **c** whose

3. That's the gym .... I go to three times a week, even when I'm busy.

   a what   **b** where   **c** which

4. The nutritionist .... ideas I'm interested in has just published a new book.

   a whose   **b** whom   **c** which

5. There aren't many days .... I don't go jogging in the park.

   a which   **b** where   **c** when

6. By the time I was 12, there weren't many sports .... I hadn't tried.

   a what   **b** which   **c** who

7. The stadium in .... I train once a week is in the north of the city.

   a which   **b** where   **c** whose

8. People don't understand .... I have to do to maintain this level of fitness.

   a which   **b** what   **c** that

Complete the sentences with a relative pronoun (*who, which, when*) and your own ideas.

1. There aren't many days .... I don't ....

2. By the time I was ten, there weren't many ....
   I hadn't tried.

3. A sports person .... I admire is ....

4. .... is a country .... I would like to visit.

☑ **Exam facts**

- In this part, you read a text with eight gaps in it.
- You have to write a word that fits each gap.

© Cambridge University Press and UCLES 2015

Education and study

1   **Complete the sentences with a linking word or phrase from the box.**

as long as	although	as well as	despite	in order to
	owing to	therefore	whereas	

1. .... you concentrate, you should pass the exam.

2. .... she always handed in her homework late, the quality of her work was high.

3. Simona took notes during the lecture .... recording what the teacher said.

4. Mike decided to get a summer job in France .... improve his French.

5. .... being one of the most intelligent students in the class, Michael's exam result was disappointing.

6. The students found that they had a free morning .... the cancellation of the lecture.

7. 'You just don't practise enough,' said the teacher, 'and .... you're not likely to improve'.

8. .... Tom wrote his essay in an hour, John needed a whole day to do his.

☑ Exam task

2   **For questions 1–8, read the text below and think of the word which best fits each gap. Use only one word in each gap. There is an example at the beginning (0).**

Example: (0) *WHETHER*

Keep on learning!

It doesn't matter **(0)** .... you are still at school or in full-time employment, making the effort to learn new things is very important. Most of us have a few subjects on **(1)** .... we focus. These may be associated **(2)** .... our study or job, or sometimes a hobby. **(3)** .... it is obviously important to develop a deep understanding of **(4)** .... matters to us most, it is equally worthwhile to extend our range of knowledge beyond what we are familiar with, and that is true at **(5)** .... age.

So the best advice is to find the time to **(6)** .... on new challenges and learn new skills outside the areas where we feel most comfortable. People often choose subjects **(7)** .... as new languages, computer skills, or painting. If you can't get to a class, then you can go online. Online courses can easily **(8)** .... found, and learning online means you put in as much time as you want each day.

3a Choose the verb that does NOT make a correct collocation with each noun.

1. *make / sit / take / do* an exam
2. *take / enrol on / apply / do* a course
3. *obtain / get / have / study* a qualification
4. *attend / leave / miss / pass* school
5. *drop / study / obtain / fail* a subject
6. *go into / graduate from / drop out of / apply to* university
7. *attend / take / skip / set* a class
8. *make / set / do / hand in* homework

3b Complete the questions with an appropriate verb from exercise 3a. Then ask and answer the questions with a partner.

1. When was the last time you .... an exam? Did you pass?
2. Do you usually .... your homework on time?
3. Have you ever .... a course in a language other than English? If not, would you like to?
4. From what age do children .... school in your country? At what age can they .... ?

☑ **Exam tips**

- Look at what comes before and after each gap and decide what kind of word you need to write – for example a pronoun, verb, preposition, etc.
- You must only write one word in each gap.
- When you have finished, read through the whole text again to make sure it makes sense.

Family and friends

1a Complete the sentences with the pronouns in the box.

me	mine	my	myself

1. I wanted my father to repair my car but in the end I did it ....
2. I was surprised to find out that my new friend's family is much bigger than ....
3. .... dancing was so funny that my friends couldn't stop laughing.
4. My mother told .... I should help her more with the housework.

1b Complete the text with the correct pronouns.

My friend and I met in **(1)** .... first year at university. We always help **(2)** .... other when we have problems of any kind. In fact, we talk every day even if we are really busy with other things. A friendship like **(3)** .... is special. I know lots of people who have lost contact with friends they met at university, and that's sad. They should ask **(4)** .... how they let that happen.

☑ Exam task

2 For questions 1–8, read the text below and think of the word which best fits each gap. Use only one word in each gap. There is an example at the beginning (0).

Example: (0) *ABOUT*

The importance of friendship

It is undeniable that friendship is important for just **(0)** .... everyone. Individuals with several close friends are usually happier than those **(1)** .... Good friends often know things that family members may not be aware of, even **(2)** .... they have lived together for years. This is probably **(3)** .... when in the company of a good friend we share our secrets and dreams. Friends turn to one **(4)** .... for suggestions on how to solve their problems. There is a tendency **(5)** .... close friends to be very honest, sometimes saying things the other person may not want to hear!

Good friends stick together, and the best relationships may last a lifetime. It is **(6)** .... surprise that most friends have similar personalities, which reduces the risk of conflict. However, people don't always have an accurate picture of **(7)** .... their true friends are. Research shows that in a surprising number of cases a person someone considers a good friend doesn't feel the **(8)** .... about them.

3a Complete the sentences with the correct form of the phrasal verbs in the box.

break up	bring up	count on	fall out	get on with
	get together	look up to	take after	

1. Mario .... everyone in his family except his older brother.
2. Everyone decided to .... to celebrate Katy's graduation, even her cousins who live in Canada.
3. My parents decided to move to London because they thought it would be easier to .... my brothers and I in a big city.
4. Everyone says I .... my father; people are always pointing out the similarities in the way we look and behave.
5. In my last year at university I .... with my girlfriend and she got together with someone else.
6. I've known Tom for twenty years and he's my best friend; I can always .... him.
7. The two sisters .... last year and haven't spoken to each other since!
8. I .... my uncle because he's achieved so many amazing things in his life.

3b Complete the questions with the correct phrasal verb from exercise 3a. Then ask and answer the questions with a partner.

1. Do you .... everyone in your family?
2. Who do you .... most – your mother or your father?
3. How often do you .... with your friends?
4. Have you ever .... with a friend or family member? What happened?
5. Which famous people do young people in your country .... the most?

⊙ Get it right!

Look at the sentences below. Then try to correct the mistake in each one.

Some of the my other friends phoned and wrote to me.
We didn't use to have our own toys – we used to share them with ourselves.

Science and technology

1 Complete the sentences with the adjective form of the words in brackets and a suffix from the box.

| -able | -al | -ed | -ful | -ible | -ic | -ing | -ous |

1. The experiments we did in the laboratory last week were all very .... (succeed)
2. Finding a cure for the disease turned out to be much more .... than the scientists expected. (challenge)
3. Important .... research is carried out in the laboratories of the university. (science)
4. If you are doing things in the right way, the results of the experiment with those chemicals should be .... (predict)
5. To be a good scientist, you need to have a .... mind. (logic)
6. The scientific team needed to present their results in a way that was .... to the non-expert. (access)
7. I'm not .... that this latest invention will make people's lives better. (convince)
8. Some things can appear to be quite .... until scientists explain them to us. (mystery)

2 Complete the table with the correct forms of the word.

Verb	Noun	Adjective
(1)	strength	strong
prove	(2)	proven
impress	impression	(3) ....
save	(4)	safe
	effect	(5) ....
produce	product	(6) ....
	(7)	accurate
(8)	success	successful

☑ Exam task

For questions 1–8, read the text below. Use the word given in capitals at the end of some of the lines to form a word that fits in the gap in the same line. There is an example at the beginning (0).

Example: (0) *EXISTENCE*

An interesting new planet

Until recently, the (0) .... of planets outside our own solar	**EXIST**
system was difficult to prove. Now, thanks to increasingly (1)	**SENSE**
equipment, hundreds have been discovered orbiting distant stars. Recent	
(2) .... of the nearest star to Earth, Proxima Centauri, have led	**INVESTIGATE**
to a (3) .... discovery: a rocky planet similar in size to the Earth	**SIGNIFY**
which may have liquid water on its surface.	
Although the new planet is (4) .... closer to Proxima Centauri	**CONSIDER**
than the Earth is to the Sun, there is still a (5) .... of life	**POSSIBLE**
there. This is because the star is much smaller and cooler than our sun, so	
conditions on the planet may be (6) .... enough to support life.	**COMFORT**
Temperatures on the planet will be (7) .... on whether there is an	**DEPEND**
atmosphere surrounding it.	
Travelling to Proxima Centauri and exploring its planet is totally	
(8) .... at the moment. Despite it being one of the nearest stars	**REAL**
to the sun, it would take thousands of years to get there using current technology.	

4

In pairs, talk about the following statements. Do you agree or disagree with them? Give reasons for your opinions.

1. Humans will be able to visit other planets one day.
2. Life will be discovered on other planets during my lifetime.
3. Space tourism will be very popular in the future.
4. Too much money is spent on space exploration.

☑ Exam facts

- In this part, you read a text with eight gaps in it.
- For each gap, there is a word in capital letters at the end of the line.
- You have to use the word in capital letters to form a word that fits the gap.

© Cambridge University Press and UCLES 2015

Food and drink

1 Complete the sentences with a noun formed from a word in the first box and a suffix from the second box.

feel	govern	know	perform	prefer	react	similar	tired

-ance	-ence	-ing	-ion	-ity	-ledge	-ment	-ness

1. People with nut allergies have to be very careful. Even if they only eat a small amount they can have a very serious allergic ....

2. A .... between the diet in Spain and Portugal is that people in both countries eat a lot of fish and seafood.

3. My .... is that the microwave oven is the most useful invention of the twentieth century. It has made preparing food so much more convenient.

4. My sister lived in Osaka for a year, so her .... of Japanese food is really excellent.

5. I think the .... should do more to improve young people's diets and encourage them to do more exercise.

6. I have a strong .... for sweet food over savoury.

7. After drinking a cup of coffee, my .... almost completely disappeared.

8. Doctors say that a healthy diet can improve your .... in exams.

☑ Exam task

2 For questions 1–8, read the text below. Use the word given in capitals at the end of some of the lines to form a word that fits in the gap in the same line. There is an example at the beginning (0).

Example: (0) *HISTORICAL*

The first coffee shops

There is some (0) .... evidence to suggest that coffee was cultivated **HISTORY**
in Africa in the tenth century, but drinking coffee didn't become (1) .... **FASHION**
in Europe until the mid-seventeenth century, with many visitors to London claiming that
going to a coffee shop was one of the great (2) .... of life. People **PLEASE**
paid an (3) .... charge of one penny to enter a coffee shop, to enjoy **ADMIT**
the supposedly (4) .... effects of the drink. Doctors at the time **BENEFIT**
believed it could cure several diseases, and many drinkers reported that coffee made
them more (5) .... and improved their mood. **ENERGY**

(6) ...., a visit to a coffee shop had a serious purpose too, as people started **INCREASE**
to meet there to discuss politics and new ideas. Good behaviour was essential and
if you were (7) ...., you could be thrown out of a shop. However, coffee **POLITE**
shops in Europe declined in popularity in the late eighteenth century due to the
greater (8) .... of tea, a drink that was easier to make than coffee. **CONSUME**

3a Complete the sentences with the noun form of the verb in brackets. Think carefully about the spelling, as the final letter or letters of the verb will change when forming a noun.

1. We had an .... about the best way to cook the food. (argue)
2. Cooking well requires a lot of .... (imagine)
3. I have no .... of giving up chocolate. I love it too much! (intend)
4. A global .... of people's diets shows that many people eat too much sugar. (analyse)
5. The .... of an important new book about healthy diets is good news. (publish)
6. In .... with the cuisine of my country, Indian food is very spicy. (compare)
7. When I listened to a .... of the dinner, I started to feel really hungry. (describe)
8. I have a strong .... for Chinese tea over European tea, which I find a bit strong. (prefer)

3b The nouns in the table have been formed from verbs. Write the verb next to each noun.

Verb	Noun
(1)	consideration
(2)	appearance
(3)	timing
(4)	confusion
(5)	arrangement
(6)	behaviour
(7)	survival
(8)	response

☑ *Exam tips*

- Look at the words before and after each gap and decide what kind of word you need to write – for example a noun, verb, adjective, adverb, etc.
- You may only have to make one change to the word in capital letters, or you may have to make two or more changes.
- If you need to write an adjective or adverb, does it need to be positive or negative? To make an adjective or adverb negative, you usually need to add a prefix.

The natural world

1 ▶ **Complete the second sentence in each pair with a negative form of the word in bold in the first sentence.**

1. We don't have much **accurate** information about the habits of this rare animal.
   Unfortunately, our information about this rare animal is probably ....

2. Most local residents **approve** of the decision to open a new park.
   Most local residents .... of the decision to close the local park.

3. The measures taken to protect the wildlife in the area are **adequate**.
   The measures taken to protect the wildlife in the area are ....

4. Few areas of the country were **affected** by the floods.
   Few areas of the country were .... by the floods.

5. The **appearance** of a very rare bird in the park caused great excitement.
   The .... of the very rare bird from the region was very disappointing.

6. Your plans to ban cars from the national park aren't very **practical**.
   Your plans to ban cars from the national park are ....

7. The children **behaved** very well when they visited the aquarium.
   Unfortunately, the children .... when they visited the aquarium.

8. The results of the survey on butterfly numbers have **encouraged** conservationists.
   The results of the survey on butterfly numbers have .... conservationists.

2 ▶ **Complete the sentences with the negative form of the adjectives in brackets. Each adjective is formed using a prefix (e.g. un-, im-).**

1. Hunting is .... in the national park and those who disobey the law will be punished. (legal)

2. Many people are .... with the air quality in the town and think it should be improved. (satisfy)

3. Some scientists fear that the environmental damage caused by global warming is .... (reverse)

4. The .... birds look very different from the adults of the same species. (mature)

5. It would be highly .... for people today to do nothing about the threats to natural habitats such as rainforests. (responsible)

6. The scientists studied two insects and found they were completely .... in terms of behaviour, size and habitat. (similar)

7. The loss of .... forests in the north of the country is very sad. (replace)

8. I couldn't read my friend's biology lecture notes because they were completely .... ! (legible)

☑ **Exam task**

For questions 1–8, read the text below. Use the word given in capitals at the end of some of the lines to form a word that fits in the gap in the same line. There is an example at the beginning (0).

Example: (0) *EXCEPTION*

Lake Titicaca

Lake Titicaca is the largest lake in South America with the **(0)** .... **EXCEPT**
of Lake Maracaibo in Venezuela, which unlike Titicaca is connected directly to the
sea. It is 190 kilometres long and reaches a maximum **(1)** .... of **DEEP**
284 metres. Approximately 60 per cent of the lake lies in Peru and the rest in Bolivia.
The lake is famous for a variety of **(2)** .... wildlife, including a **USUAL**
giant frog that can weigh up to three kilogrammes.
Some animals in the lake are **(3)** .... species, which led to the **DANGER**
(4) .... of Titicaca National Reserve in 1978. The protection of the **ESTABLISH**
wildlife is guaranteed, and so is the beautiful scenery that makes a visit to the lake
so **(5)** .... **FORGET**
There are numerous islands on the lake, although not all are **(6)** .... **ACCESS**
to tourists. The **(7)** .... of some of the islands are known as the **INHABIT**
Uros people, who still maintain their traditional way of life, but at the same time
welcome visitors. **(8)** ...., this beautiful lake is often ignored **SURPRISE**
by tourists.

Write the adjectives and verbs with negative prefixes from exercises 1, 2 and 3 in the table.

dis-	il-	im-	in-	ir-	mis-	un-

 Get it right!

Look at the sentence below. Then try to correct the mistake.

Nowadays, zoos are considered by many people to be unuseful and cruel.

Travel and holidays

1 **Match the uses of the present simple and present continuous with the example sentences.**

1. To describe a temporary situation	**a** Unless you work harder, you won't be successful.
2. To describe a daily routine	**b** I'm seeing my best friend Jessica at the weekend.
3. To describe a current activity	**c** My husband's always losing his car keys.
4. To describe a possible consequence in a conditional sentence	**d** The coach to Liverpool leaves at 7.10 in the morning.
5. To describe a timetable for travel	**e** I'm working on an important project at the moment.
6. To describe a habit or repeated action	**f** I usually take a long walk in the morning.
7. To state scientific rules or principles	**g** I'm living in my brother's flat until I find my own place.
8. To describe plans and arrangements	**h** Water boils at 100 degrees Celsius.

2 **Complete the second sentence so it has a similar meaning to the first. Use one or two words.**

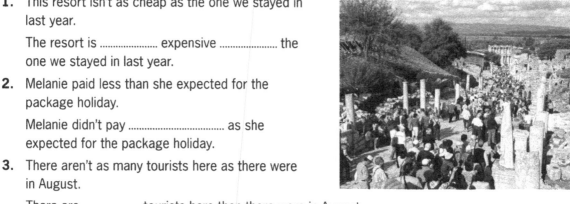

1. This resort isn't as cheap as the one we stayed in last year.

   The resort is .... expensive .... the one we stayed in last year.

2. Melanie paid less than she expected for the package holiday.

   Melanie didn't pay .... as she expected for the package holiday.

3. There aren't as many tourists here as there were in August.

   There are .... tourists here than there were in August.

4. There is more time to appreciate a country's culture if you go on a guided tour there.

   There is .... time to appreciate a country's culture if you don't go on a guided tour there.

5. Bianca isn't as fluent in Chinese as her friend.

   Bianca doesn't speak Chinese .... as her friend.

6. Emma didn't look at the pictures in the museum as carefully as her friend did.

   Emma looked .... at the pictures in the museum than her friend did.

7. There are fewer historic buildings in this town than in other places we've visited.

   There aren't .... historic buildings in this town as in other places we've visited.

8. Compared to other places in the region, this isn't a very beautiful village.

   In .... with other places in the region, this isn't a very beautiful village.

3

For questions 1–6, complete the second sentence so that it has a similar meaning to the first sentence, using the word given. Do not change the word given. You must use between two and five words, including the word given. Here is an example (0).

Example:

0   On holiday I prefer going sightseeing to relaxing on the beach.

RATHER

On holiday I ...*would rather go sightseeing than*... relax on the beach.

1.   Nobody explained why the flight had been delayed.

REASON

Nobody gave .... to the flight.

2.   Last year's skiing holiday was more exciting than this year's holiday by the sea.

AS

This year's holiday by the sea .... last year's skiing holiday.

3.   Maria doesn't think we should visit the museum because it's not very interesting.

POINT

Maria says .... the museum because it's not very interesting.

4.   All of us are excited about our trip to China next month.

LOOKING

Everyone .... our trip to China next month.

5.   When I was in Sweden, I managed to learn some Swedish.

PICK

When I was in Sweden, I was .... some Swedish.

6.   The architecture here makes me think of the buildings in Amsterdam.

REMINDS

The architecture here .... of the buildings in Amsterdam.

- In this part, there are six pairs of sentences with a word in capital letters.
- Part of the second sentence of each pair is missing.
- You have to complete the second sentence using the word in capital letters so that it has a similar meaning to the first sentence.

© Cambridge University Press and UCLES 2015

Daily life

1 Change the statements in the first sentences into reported speech.

1. 'I'll meet you at seven,' John promised his sister.

   John promised his sister

   .... at seven.

2. 'You've arrived late to work twice this week,' the manager said to Lucas.

   The manager said to Lucas that

   .... late to work twice that week.

3. 'I'm going on a business trip to Japan,' Rachel told her friend.

   Rachel told her friend that .... on a business trip to Japan.

4. 'If we leave now, we won't be late,' George told Jessica.

   George told Jessica that if .... late.

5. 'We'll have to tidy up the house,' Micah said to his brother.

   Micah told his brother that .... tidy up the house.

6. 'I have a lot of work experience,' the man said at the job interview.

   At the job interview, the man said .... a lot of work experience.

☑ Exam task

2 For questions 1–6, complete the second sentence so that it has a similar meaning to the first sentence, using the word given. Do not change the word given. You must use between two and five words, including the word given. Here is an example (0).

Example:

0 It's not a problem for Tom if he has to take the train to work.

MIND

Tom ....*doesn't mind taking*............ the train to work.

1. Going to bed early has a big effect on how Leila feels the next morning.

DIFFERENCE

If Leila goes to bed early, it .... how she feels the next morning.

2. Even though Max took the early bus, he was still late for work.

FACT

Max was still late for work in .... he took the early bus.

3. Last year I decided I wouldn't eat fast food for lunch any more.

GIVE

Last year I decided .... fast food for lunch.

4. Melanie goes jogging and answers her important emails before breakfast.

WELL

Melanie goes jogging .... her important emails before breakfast.

5. My television needs fixing as soon as possible.

GET

I must .... as soon as possible

6. Clara says she doesn't usually go out at the weekend.

UNUSUAL

Clara says it .... go out at the weekend.

3a **Complete the second sentence so that it means the same as the first. Pay particular attention to the word order.**

1. 'Do you know where my car keys are?' Tom asked his wife.

Tom asked his wife if she knew ....

2. 'Are you going to the party?' Melissa asked Paola.

Melissa asked Paola whether ....

3. 'Have you been to the new department store?' Peter's friend asked him.

Peter's friend asked him whether ....

4. 'Will you be late home on Tuesday?' Alex's father asked him.

Alex's father asked him whether ....

3b **Read the reported questions and write the direct questions.**

1. Lee's boss asked him if he was willing to work on Saturday.

....

2. Lee's wife asked him if he could do the shopping on his way home.

....

3. Lee asked his son if he wanted to play football in the garden.

....

4. Lee asked his friend how long he had been off work.

....

☑) **Exam tips**

- This part often tests your knowledge of phrasal verbs and set phrases.
- Underline the part of the first sentence that corresponds to the gap in the second sentence.
- You mustn't change the word in capital letters.

Weather

☑ Exam task

1 For questions 1–6, complete the second sentence so that it has a similar meaning to the first sentence, using the word given. Do not change the word given. You must use between two and five words, including the word given. Here is an example (0).

Example:

0 We couldn't go sailing because there wasn't enough wind.

LACK

Due .... *to the lack of wind* ...., we couldn't go sailing.

1. Some schools were closed for a couple of days because of the heavy snow.

LED

The heavy snow .... for a couple of days.

2. Steve doesn't take much notice of the weather forecast.

ATTENTION

Steve doesn't .... the weather forecast.

3. John wishes he had taken an umbrella to work this morning.

TAKING

John .... an umbrella to work this morning.

4. Donna said that apart from Friday, every day last week had been really hot.

EXCEPTION

Donna said that .... Friday, every day last week had been really hot.

5. This is the worst weather we've ever had in July.

AS

We've .... as this in July.

6. I'm sure it was unbearably hot where you were staying.

MUST

The .... unbearable where you were staying.

2 Complete the sentences with the correct phrasal verb from the box.

get away	keep up with	make out	put off
put up with	set off	soak up	turn out

1. We decided to .... our trip to the beach until the weather improved.
2. I had problems .... the buildings in the distance because of the thick fog.
3. I find it hard to .... days and days of wet weather.
4. It was so hot I couldn't .... the better runners in the race.
5. We .... very early before it got too hot.
6. It .... to be a very nice day after a cloudy start.
7. At this time of the year, people want to .... and visit a warmer country.
8. Aunt Mary is outside in the garden .... the sun.

3 Complete the sentences with the correct form of the verb in brackets.

1. If you .... (go) to the coast at this time of year, it will probably be quite cool.
2. If he .... (take) a coat and umbrella, he wouldn't have got wet.
3. Unless people take more action to reduce CO_2 emissions, the problems associated with global warming (get) .... worse.
4. If I .... (spend) more time in the sun, I'd have a lovely tan.
5. If we'd had more rain last year, our village's crops .... (be) better.
6. Unless the weather forecast .... (be) wrong, there won't be any more snow today.
7. If we left early, we .... (miss) the bad weather.
8. If I haven't got sun screen, I .... (be able) to lie on the beach for long.

(o) Get it right!

Look at the sentences below and choose the correct one.

She asked herself what would have happened if she hadn't caught that bus.

She asked herself what had happened if she wouldn't have caught that bus.

Science and technology

☑ Exam task

1 You are going to read an article about new technology and students. For questions 1–6, choose the answer (A, B, C or D) which you think fits best according to the text.

Student life and technology

By Debra Mallin, a business student at Greyfort University

Last Saturday, as my grandfather drove me and my sister home from a dinner to celebrate his birthday, he got frustrated at not being able to remember the name of the singer of a song he'd just heard on the radio. Without a second thought, I grabbed my smartphone, searched for the song and found the name, Bob Dylan. For me and my friends, this is a completely natural course of action, but it totally astonished my grandfather, who didn't understand how I had checked the information so quickly. My sister and I laughed and explained, but afterwards, it made me think about how much I depend on technology.

The list of the ways I use technology is endless: writing, planning, socialising, communicating and shopping, to name a few. When I reflected on its impact on my education, I saw that, for my fellow students and I, technology has been significant in many ways. Returning to the story of my grandfather and the smartphone, he had asked me more about how I used it and about university life. He said he thought we had an easy life compared to previous generations. My sister caught my eye and we exchanged a smile. But whereas she was thinking our grandfather was just being a typical 65-year-old, I could see his point.

Not only are we lucky enough to have the same educational benefits as those of previous generations, we have so many more as well. We still have walk-in libraries available to us, and I can see why some students choose to find and use resources in these distraction-free locations. However, the only option for studying used to be sitting in these libraries with as many books from your reading list as you could find, yet now a single search for your chosen study topic online can immediately provide access to a huge range of resources. At universities, interaction between students and university staff is another area that has changed considerably with developments in technology. We can have face-to-face time with our

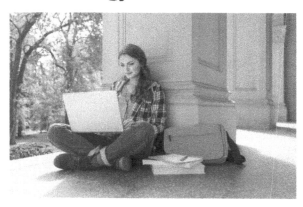

tutors when we need it, and also communicate using our electronic gadgets from the comfort of our homes, or on the bus. The most popular means of doing this is via instant messaging or social media – email is often considered too slow, and it has become unacceptable for messages to be unanswered for any length of time. While this puts an extra strain on the university's academic support team, who usually have to answer the queries as they come in, we students are greatly benefitted.

It's important that we remember to appreciate how much the advances in technology have given us. Electronic devices such as tablets, smartphones, and laptops are now standard equipment in most classrooms and lecture halls, and why shouldn't they be? The replacement of textbooks with tablets allows students the luxury of having up-to-date, interactive and even personalised learning materials, with the added benefit of them not costing the earth.

When we compare the student life of the past and that of the present day, it is tempting to focus on the obvious differences when it comes to technology. In actual fact, students are doing what they've always done: embracing the resources available and adapting them in ways which allow them to work more efficiently and to live more enjoyably. The pace of change in technology continuously gathers speed, so we have to value each innovation as it happens.

1. What does the writer illustrate by describing the incident in the car?

   A the older generation's frustration at people's dependence on technology

   B how unaware young people are of some effects of technology

   C the difference in attitudes to technology between two generations

   D how technology helps different generations communicate

2. What did the writer think of her grandfather's comment, mentioned in the second paragraph?

   A It showed how out-of-date he was.

   B It had an element of truth in it.

   C It was an annoying thing to say.

   D It made her feel sorry for him.

3. What does the writer say about getting study resources from libraries?

   A She considers libraries more preferable places for study than home.

   B She cannot understand why anyone chooses to go to a library now.

   C She appreciates the fact that people can still study in libraries if they want to.

   D She thinks libraries are limited by the quantity of resources they can store.

4. What disadvantage of new technology does the writer mention in the third paragraph?

   A Those who can afford the best gadgets gain an unfair advantage.

   B Sometimes slow internet connections make communication difficult.

   C A heavier workload is created for teaching staff at the university.

   D Students cannot escape from dealing with university issues.

5. What is the purpose of the question 'Why shouldn't they be?' in the fourth paragraph?

   A to express an opinion

   B to introduce some problems

   C to make a criticism

   D to indicate uncertainty

6. What is the writer's conclusion about students today in the final paragraph?

   A They have such different lives to previous generations that it's unwise to compare them.

   B They deal better with change than previous generations did.

   C They take advantage of new resources more quickly than previous generations did.

   D They are behaving in a similar way to previous generations of students.

---

2 Complete the sentences with a phrase. Use one word from each box for each phrase.

back	hard	high-	instant	interactive	search	social	virtual

drive	engine	games	media	messaging	reality	tech	up

1. Google is the most used .... in the world.

2. I don't text my friends any more because .... is so much faster.

3. How much storage space is left on the .... in your PC?

4. If you don't .... your work, you are in danger of losing it.

5. The car's .... steering system is unique.

6. Play the .... on our website to learn more about science and technology.

7. .... makes you feel as if you are in a real three-dimensional space.

8. By using .... like Twitter, you can communicate with anyone on the internet.

☑ *Exam facts*

- In this part, you read a long text.
- You have to choose the correct answer (A, B, C or D) for six questions.

House and home

 Exam task

1 You are going to read a review of a TV programme about homes of the future. For questions 1–6, choose the answer (A, B, C or D) which you think fits best according to the text.

The homes of the future viewed from today

Mark Finchley reviews TV series _Tomorrow's Homes_
Having just watched the whole of Channel 8's TV series _Tomorrow's Homes_, I've been wondering about how anyone can predict the future of domestic life. You'd imagine that if you knew what architects and technology companies were developing now to make life easier, more exciting and more beautiful, you'd have a pretty good idea of what to expect in tomorrow's homes. In reality, it's more complicated, and just as much about what we'll choose to hang on to from **today's** – the things that are 'future-proof'. In the 1950s, people thought that in the twenty-first century household tasks would be done by labour-saving devices or robots – with food pills for dinner. Yet people still wash up and cook, even though the technology exists that makes neither of these tasks necessary.

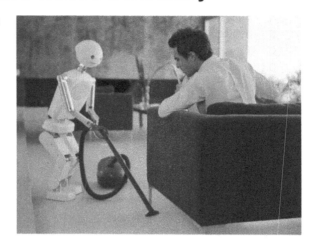

Tomorrow's Homes, however, dared to make predictions which it turned into reality using an average home belonging to a family called the Forseys. Four miles of cable were installed in the house so that all the electrics, from lights to the fridge, could be controlled via the internet, and various other devices and gadgets were introduced in addition to this. The family were then filmed as they got used to their new home life. Programme presenter Harry Thwaites is also a consultant who spends his work life imagining the future, so testing out his ideas for the programme was a fascinating experiment for him. His approach was to use technology that was not totally brand new, but had only recently become more affordable. CCTV cameras for security have been around for years, for example, but they are no longer only an option for the mega-rich.

The Forsey family consists of a husband and wife with four children and two grandchildren. They appear to be very natural and ordinary on the programme, and it was always interesting to see how they reacted to

the technology they were testing. One example that **sticks** in the mind is when Janine, the mother, enters her reconstructed, all-white home (after successfully unlocking her new front door by using her thumb print as a key), and she immediately bursts into tears – quite understandably it has to be said. A short while later, her husband Ben gets locked out because the skin on his thumb is too rough. As the series progresses, however, they slowly come to accept the technology, and even start to believe it could have some value in their lives.

I was keen to see during the show if anything emerged as potentially future-proof, and there were some great examples. To help Janine deal with various worries, she was provided with a mind-controlled relaxation tool. This was a kind of headband connected to a DVD, which, incredibly, she could control with her thoughts. When she relaxed mentally, she made an image of the sun go down, as it would at night, on the DVD. When she had tried the gadget and achieved the sun set, she was asked how effective the gadget had been. Janine commented, 'Nothing can compare to a nice cup of tea and a good soap opera!'

1. The writer makes the point in the first paragraph that predicting how homes will be in the future
   A requires detailed study of architectural trends.
   B is impossible if you only look at new developments.
   C has been very difficult until now.
   D is made easier by programmes and articles about them in the media.

2. What does 'today's' refer to in the first paragraph?
   A current ideas
   B the present reality
   C the homes we currently live in
   D modern architecture

3. According to the second paragraph, the technology installed in the Forseys' house
   A was chosen to match the specific needs of the family.
   B was previously only used by a limited section of the population.
   C was still too expensive for anybody except the wealthiest.
   D was tried out by experts before the family used it.

4. What does 'sticks' mean in the third paragraph?
   A blocks something
   B remains there
   C corrects an error
   D highlights something

5. According to the third paragraph, how did the family members react to the new technology?
   A Their attitude towards it became increasingly positive.
   B Some of them adjusted more quickly to it than others.
   C The parents struggled with it throughout the series.
   D Some of their responses to it were surprising.

6. How did Janine feel about the mind-controlled relaxation tool?
   A She was amazed at what it was capable of.
   B She thought it would work if used with other things.
   C She found it totally useless.
   D She preferred more traditional methods of relaxation.

2 Complete the text with the correct alternatives.

What will our homes be like in 2030?

There are some things that we cannot predict about the world in 2030, but others seem certain. For example, we are definitely **(1)** *going to have / having* many more homes in larger cities as the world's population **(2)** *will be continuing / continues* to grow. But what will these homes be like?

Firstly, 'The Internet of Things' **(3)** *will have been / will be* an established part of everyone's lives by then. All electronic devices in your home will be connected, and they **(4)** *are communicating / will be communicating* with each other constantly.

By 2030, you also **(5)** *will have equipped / will be equipped* your house with smart technology, so you'll have movement, temperature and humidity sensors throughout the house. These **(6)** *will be measuring / will have measured* the environment in your house constantly. In fact, they **(7)** *can even / will even be able* to tell you if you've left a door open, or a tap on!

☑ **Exam tips**

- Quickly read through the text before you answer the questions to get an idea of what it is about.
- Read through all the questions so that you know what you need to look for in the text.
- Don't assume an option is correct just because you see the same words in the text. You should make sure the general meaning of the option is expressed in the text.

Work

 Exam task

1 You are going to read an article about some amazing jobs. For questions 1–6, choose the answer (A, B, C or D) which you think fits best according to the text.

Dream Jobs

By Giovanni Marks

During our teens, all the pupils at my school had to have a meeting with a 'careers advisor' who only seemed to know about jobs at the local ship-building works. That was fine for some, but many of us would have liked to hear about a wider range of opportunities at that time. If only she had known about the jobs I've been researching for this article! It seems there are positions out there that are almost too good to be true.

Take, for example, the job with the title 'Ice cream flavour advisor' for ice cream manufacturer Frederick's. Imagine making and tasting ice cream for a living! From the Fredrick's website I learned that the people who do this job are all chefs and food scientists, and often go on what they call 'taste hunts' where they travel to other countries, trying new foods to get inspiration for new products. The website's home page also states that 'every ingredient deserves consideration', meaning anything from peanuts to potatoes could make it into the next flavour advisor's invention. I guess the one downside of this job could be tasting failed creations.

For those worried about the health implications of eating so much ice cream, then how about something more active? The perfect job for water sports lovers was advertised in 2015 by holiday company Travel Now. They needed a water slide tester! This involved getting into swimming gear and speeding down slides at various holiday centres around the world to check for any issues. The company was seeking applicants with strong written and verbal skills, experience in social media and a willingness to travel.

Another job that seems impossibly wonderful is one for those who dream of living on a remote island. As the caretaker of a private island in the Maldives, Simon Grainger gets to enjoy fabulous weather, fishing and boating as part of his job. However, he says that while it may sound more like an extended holiday than work, the responsibilities of the job can be very demanding. These include maintaining and repairing the island owners' property and cleaning up after storms. On top of that,

being by yourself on an island means that your social life suffers. Seeing friends involves an hour's boat ride, which is never easy and sometimes impossible. Grainger warns anyone considering a job like his to be realistic about it. He explains you've got be very practical with good physical fitness, and happy in your own company. If you are this type of person, you'll do the job well and never want to go back to life on the mainland.

A fortune cookie is a moon-shaped biscuit given away in Chinese restaurants that contains a little piece of paper with a message on it. Millions of these are read every day, but few realise that people actually get paid to write the words of wisdom you find when you crack your cookie open. Daisy Cheng, president of New Asian Food in Los Angeles, used to be **one such person**. It wasn't exactly her chosen career path, it was more of a role she fell into. When the company expanded and realised they needed to update their cookie messages, she was asked to do it because her English language skills were stronger than other employees'. She found it difficult to start with, but soon she was finding inspiration everywhere, from subway signs to newspapers.

As a writer myself, I would love to create messages for fortune cookies, but I would be delighted to do any one of these amazing jobs. Listen up careers advisors!

1. How does the writer feel about the careers advisor he met when he was younger?
   - **A** He regrets that she was unable to help any of the teenagers.
   - **B** He found her guidance quite useful at the time.
   - **C** He thought it was unnecessary to see her.
   - **D** He wishes she had been aware of a greater variety of job options.

2. What is claimed on the website for Frederick's ice cream?
   - **A** There is no food type that they will refuse to experiment with.
   - **B** They are able to make most ingredients taste good in ice cream.
   - **C** They trial every new flavour creation internationally before it goes on sale.
   - **D** No other ice cream producer has greater expertise.

3. Applicants for the job of water slide tester were required by Travel Now to
   - **A** be good at communicating with people.
   - **B** have plenty of travel experience.
   - **C** have good IT qualifications.
   - **D** be very physically fit.

4. What does Grainger say about his role as caretaker on a private island?
   - **A** He is considering giving it up so he can move back to the mainland.
   - **B** The only thing that is hard about it is being alone on the island.
   - **C** It might not be the right job for everyone.
   - **D** The holiday lifestyle involved is not always enjoyable.

5. What does the fifth paragraph say about Daisy Cheng getting her job as fortune cookie writer?
   - **A** She did not deliberately choose to do the job.
   - **B** She got the job because none of her colleagues spoke any English.
   - **C** She applied for it when the company grew and needed more people to do the job.
   - **D** She tried to avoid doing the job at first.

6. What does 'one such person' refer to in the fifth paragraph?
   - **A** someone who is a company vice president
   - **B** someone from New York
   - **C** someone who didn't know fortune cookie message writers existed
   - **D** someone who writes the messages in fortune cookies

---

2 **Complete the second sentence so that it has a similar meaning to the first sentence, using the word given in bold.**

1. I will hopefully get a promotion this year. **HOPE**

   ....

2. Josh lost his job because he was late so many times. **IF ONLY**

   ....

3. Kathy is a nurse but she wants to be a doctor. **WISHES**

   ....

4. Mark is talking about going to work abroad. I would be sad if he did. **HOPE**

   ....

5. The new boss is Nick Jones. Everyone would prefer Leo Patten. **WISHES**

   ....

6. Most employers don't give employees eight weeks' holiday a year. I wish they did! **IF ONLY**

   ....

 Get it right!

Look at the sentence below. Then try to correct the mistake.

I wish you were there; it was fantastic!

☑ *Exam task*

1 You are going to read an article about a national vote for people's favourite tree. Six sentences have been removed from the article. Choose from the sentences A–G the one which fits each gap (1–6). There is one extra sentence which you do not need to use.

Tree of the Year

The aim of the national Tree of the Year competition is to promote and celebrate the most interesting trees around the country. Images and descriptions of a shortlist of 28 trees are put online and the public are asked to vote for their favourite.

The four trees that gain the most votes before 5 p.m. on 5th October will be given a grant of £1,000. In addition, all trees that receive 1,000 or more votes will get a grant of £500. The grants may be spent on a tree health check or advice from a tree expert, or an educational event, for example. [1]

Among the 28 shortlisted trees there are a wide range of tree species, each with its own unique, fascinating story. For example, the 'Ding Dong' tree is a copper beech tree growing in a primary school playground. It was named the 'Ding Dong' tree because of a game pupils invented in which they race to touch its trunk, shouting 'Ding Dong!' The protective space underneath the 50-year-old tree is used as a magical outdoor classroom, while the indoor classroom displays pictures of the tree through each season of the year. [2]

Many of the other trees in the competition are remarkable for their age alone. The Craigends Yew, for example, is thought to be up to 700 years old, making it one of the oldest in Scotland. It is an amazing sight as many of its branches have layered. [3] As a result of these extra growths, the total size when measured around the tree's crown (the main body of its leaves and branches) is a massive 100 metres.

Another very old tree, the Holm Oak in Kilbroney Park, Northern Ireland, is much loved by local people. It measures 3.6 metres around the trunk, and its beautiful bark looks like the skin of a snake. [4] The advantage of this lack of uprightness is that young children can climb safely and easily on it. Kilbroney Park is home to many remarkable trees, but this tree was chosen as the favourite by community members.

A 500-year-old veteran oak tree stands in the ancient woodland pasture at Carngafallt in Wales. One of the interesting things about this twisted, hollow tree is that it has several 'air trees' growing out of it. An 'air tree' is one growing without its roots touching the ground. [5] It extends its roots down inside the oak's hollow trunk.

The original Bramley apple tree in Nottinghamshire is younger than many in this competition, but is the famous parent of all modern Bramley apple trees. [6] Many years later, Matthew Bramley, the new owner of the tree, was carrying some of his fruit when he met a gardener called Henry Merryweather. Henry asked if he could take some cuttings from Matthew's trees to grow his own trees. Mr Bramley agreed, provided they were named 'Bramley's Seedling'.

A This means that they are touching the ground and have taken root.

B These roots have become enormous with age and have now emerged above the ground. Children love to jump over them like horses in a race.

C But the most distinctive thing about this tree is that its main trunk is leaning towards the ground at an angle of 45 degrees.

D The best example of this on the big old tree is another species of tree called a rowan.

E Alternatively, they could be used to hold a community event in honour of the tree.

F It was planted from a seed in 1809 by a woman called Ann Brailsford.

G Children hang bird feeders from its branches and it is used as the focus of many of the educational activities going on around it.

---

2 ▶ Complete the sentences in the notice with the correct alternatives.

BLUE RIDGE FOREST RULES

1. Under no circumstances *should / need* fires be lit in the forest.

2. Only walkers *may / need* use the routes marked with yellow arrows.

3. Dogs *do not have to / must not* be on their leads in the West Lane area of the forest.

4. You *must not / need not* push, carry or use a bicycle on any forest footpath.

5. Children *should not / do not have to* be allowed to climb young trees.

6. All rubbish *should / may* be taken home.

7. Find out about which areas of the forest you *must / can* enter on factsheet 112.

8. Walkers *must not / do not have to* stay on the marked paths, but it is advisable that they do.

☑ *Exam facts*

- In this part, you read a long text with six gaps in it.
- There is a list of sentences (A–G).
- You have to choose the sentence that fits each gap.
- There is one extra sentence that you do not need to use.

☑ **Exam task**

1 You are going to read an article about how a desert marathon runner found a pet dog. Six sentences have been removed from the article. Choose from the sentences A–G the one which fits each gap (1–6). There is one extra sentence which you do not need to use.

The desert runner and the dog

The story of how a homeless dog became an internet star and found a home in the UK begins in China, in the Gobi Desert, during an ultramarathon in which competitors cross 250 kilometres of desert in seven days. The dog 'adopted' Australian **marathon** runner Dion Leonard when it chose to join the racers on the second day. Leonard's affection for the dog grew as it ran hour after hour with him in the harsh desert conditions, and by the last **stage** of the race, they could not be separated. He named her Gobi, after the desert.

1 _____ He claims she helped him do so well in the race. In fact, Gobi set the **pace** for Leonard, and the two days she didn't run with him, his times were not as fast as when she did. He added that she sometimes **beat** him too – but when Gobi ran too quickly she would stop and wait for him to **catch up**, and then they would continue together.

Dion Leonard's affection for the dog was so strong that he decided he would take her back to Scotland, where he currently lives. **2** _____ This included setting up a crowdfunding campaign (raising many small amounts of money from a large number of people) on the internet to cover the costs of medical and **fitness** checks for Gobi and for her to be flown to Scotland.

However, the drama of the story increased when Gobi disappeared just before she was due to travel to Beijing. **3** _____ She had escaped by dashing outside through an open door in Urumqi, the Chinese city where some of the ultramarathon race team were caring for her.

After hearing this news, Leonard took a flight back to China as soon as he could, and began to search for Gobi. He knew there was little chance of finding Gobi on his own, so he set up a media and social media campaign, and put posters up all over the city. Soon, groups of local volunteers were helping him hunt for Gobi all across Urumqi, looking in parks and dog shelters, and asking all the people they came across whether they'd seen the dog. Leonard became quite well-known after he was interviewed by local television, and people often stopped him in the street to wish him luck and give him encouragement. **4** _____

Leonard didn't **give in**, and eventually the call that he'd been waiting for came: a man and his son had seen a small dog while **walking** their dog in a local park. **5** _____ Leonard was doubtful – the man had sent pictures, but they were a bit too dark to be able to identify the dog as Gobi.

When he walked into the room where they agreed to meet the man with the dog he'd found, Leonard was not feeling at all hopeful that it was Gobi. But as soon as the dog saw him, she rushed towards him and jumped up, barking excitedly. **6** _____ He's deeply grateful to the residents of Urumqi, as he would never have found her if they hadn't helped him in his search.

A He soon found that the process for achieving this was difficult and expensive, so he returned home and started making arrangements from there.

B They had taken her home and thought she could be Gobi.

C It was as if the two had never been apart, and Leonard says he felt just like he had when they were racing together.

D She had to be monitored there for three months before she was allowed to travel out of China.

E Leonard managed to win second place in the race, despite having to carry Gobi across rivers and giving her food and water from the supplies he had to carry.

F Furthermore, he feared the dog could easily have run a long way out into the surrounding countryside.

G Leonard even launched a live blog to keep people interested in and up-to-date with his search.

2 ▶ **Complete the sentences with a word in bold from the text in Exercise 1.**

1. Jake doesn't like .... the new puppy so I always have to do it.

2. You need a really good level of .... to be a good cyclist.

3. Always fight your match right to the end – never ....!

4. I always run alone because I like to go at my own ....

5. During the first .... of the race, the Danish swimmer was leading.

6. When we play tennis doubles against our friends, we always .... them, but they don't mind.

7. If the other competitors get too far ahead in a race, you won't be able to .... enough to win.

8. When I ran my first ...., it took me two weeks to recover!

3 ▶ **Choose the correct alternative to complete the sentences.**

1. The rules say you *must / shall* not run across another competitor's lane during the 1500 metres race.

2. At the stadium, it's great when there isn't a full crowd because they *allow / let* us sit in the better seats.

3. If you want tickets for Saturday's match, you *can / should* buy them as soon as possible.

4. Would you *mind / matter* if I didn't come to basketball practice tonight?

5. You'd *rather / better* stop cycling now if your ankle feels sore.

6. I *could / should* give you a lift back from the pool tonight if you wanted me to.

7. *Would / Do* you like the coach to give you some extra practice exercises this week?

8. *Could / Shall* we rent the football pitch for another hour, please?

☑ **Exam tips**

- Quickly read through the text to get an idea of what it is about and its structure, and read sentences A–G.

- Carefully read what comes before and after each gap.

- In sentences A–G and in the sentences before and after the gaps in the main text, underline words that link the information together – for example *them, this, that, it, also, however, although, one* and *do so*.

Education and study

Exam task

1 You are going to read an article about trips for school children. Six sentences have been removed from the article. Choose from the sentences A–G the one which fits each gap (1–6). There is one extra sentence which you do not need to use.

Field trips for school children

For many years, school children in the US have been taken on 'field trips' to cultural institutions such as museums of art and of science, as well as theatres, zoos and historical sites.

Despite these trips involving some expense and disruption to class timetables, educators arrange them in the belief that schools exist not only to teach economically useful skills, but also to produce civilised young people who appreciate the arts and culture. **1** So you could say that taking school students on field trips is a means of giving everyone equal access to their cultural heritage.

However, there have been increasing signs in recent years that the attitude towards field trips is changing, with the number of tours organised for school groups falling significantly in museums all around the country. Take the Field Museum in Chicago, for example. It used to have over 300,000 students each year through its doors. That number has dropped to below 200,000 more recently. **2** A survey exploring the trend carried out by a group of school administrators found that over half the schools they asked had decided to cancel trips planned for the next academic year.

So what are the reasons for this change? The most obvious one is the issue of finance. Because there are increasing demands on their funds (computers and sports facilities aren't cheap), schools are forced to make a difficult choice about how to spend the limited money they have. **3** A significant number of school heads also consider days spent away from school a waste of time, believing that the only worthwhile use of students' time is spent preparing for exams in the classroom.

Although school trips do still happen, the nature of these field days is also changing. Schools increasingly use trips as a treat for students who work hard, rather than as an opportunity for cultural learning. They are taken to amusement parks or sporting events instead of to museums and historical sites. **4** In a recent survey, 500 Arkansas teachers were asked about the purpose of trips they organised. Older teachers were significantly more likely to believe the primary purpose of a field trip was to provide a learning experience than younger teachers, who were more likely to view the main point of a trip as fun.

But why should anybody worry if school children go on fewer trips? Those that believe this is a negative development in education would say that cultural field trips contribute to the development of students into well-educated adults who have a healthy interest in history and the arts. **5**

One exception is the research led by Jay P. Greene at Arkansas University. His team found that students who received a tour of an art museum significantly improved their knowledge of and ability to think critically about art. **6** The researchers warn that if schools cut field trips or switch from 'reward' trips to less educational destinations, then valuable opportunities to broaden and enrich children's learning experiences are lost.

A This shift to 'reward' field trips could have a basis in generational differences between teachers' reasons for organising days out of school.

B However, there is little evidence to support this argument, as few studies into the effect of field trips have been done.

C An online tour of the museum, during which they viewed and discussed five paintings, made little impact on students.

D Faced with this dilemma, field trips are an obvious thing to cut since they are seen by many as a luxury.

E While there are parents who will take their children to cultural places and events in their free time, there are plenty of other children who will never have this kind of opportunity unless schools offer it.

F They also displayed stronger historical empathy and were more likely to visit cultural institutions in the future.

G A similar pattern is emerging in many other areas of the country, and is set to continue.

2 **Complete the sentences with an adjective, noun or adverb form of the word in brackets.**

1. The students are on an .... visit to France. (education)
2. The study found .... of an increase in numbers of migrating birds. (evident)
3. A team of eight .... worked together on the project. (research)
4. The museum is the first .... in the region to introduce free admission. (institute)
5. The writer's .... about the value of universities was very clear. (argue)
6. It has been .... proven that bulls can't see the colour red. (science)
7. The most .... thing I learned at school was always to ask questions. (value)
8. There is a good range of .... activities happening in this town. (culture)

3 **Choose the alternative for each sentence which is NOT correct.**

1. We can choose to spend a year of our course abroad, so I *must / might / may* go to China.
2. Where is Tom? He *ought to / should / would* be here for the lecture, but I can't see him.
3. He doesn't know where the information came from, so it *can't / shouldn't / needn't* be trusted.
4. These figures *may / can / must* be correct because we've checked them three times.
5. This *has / ought / needs* to be the best course for me, because it includes everything I'm interested in.
6. I think the course *could / can / might* be more challenging than I expected, but I'm not sure yet.
7. The school canteen is so large that all the pupils *should / can / may* have lunch at the same time.
8. There *shouldn't / can't / shan't* be more than 30 students in the class because that's the maximum per group.

 Get it right!

Look at the sentence below. Then try to correct the mistake.

You are doing well in your studies in science and maths and you can become a doctor one day.

Cultures and customs

1 **Complete the text and with the correct passive form of the verb in brackets.**

La Tomatina takes place each year in Buñol, a small town near Valencia in Spain. Many stories **(1)** .... (tell) about how it all started. One is that in 1945, a group of young people attending a festival grabbed tomatoes from a nearby market stall and started a playful food fight. They **(2)** .... (stop) by the police, but on the same day in August a year after that, a food battle **(3)** .... (fight) in Buñol again, with local people bringing tomatoes to throw at each other. In the 1950s the event **(4)** .... (ban), but the locals continued and **(5)** .... (lock) up in jail. The people of Buñol demonstrated against the ban, and finally in 1959 they **(6)** .... (allow) to hold the event again. However, a strict code of conduct **(7)** .... (introduce), controlling issues such as how the fight was to begin. Since then, the festival **(8)** .... (attend) by more and more people each year.

☑ Exam task

2 **You are going to read an article in which four people describe going to see an unusual annual event. For questions 1–10 choose from the people (A–D). The people may be chosen more than once.**

Which person mentions

the possibility of people at the event having their belongings stolen?	1
regretting being without an item of protective equipment?	2
the bravery of the people who took part?	3
a warning about organising a trip to the event?	4
an injury caused during the event?	5
how hard it was to get a good position to view the event?	6
products that were available to buy during the event?	7
experiencing two strongly contrasting emotions?	8
people with a particular interest who would like the event?	9
the reason why the event originally began?	10

The world's strangest annual events?

Four travellers talk about experiencing a very unusual event held annually around the world.

A Sadie Grossman

Last year, I was one of 30,000 people who took part in La Tomatina, an annual festival held in Buñol, Spain, during which townspeople and visitors fill the streets and take part in a tomato fight. I've neither laughed so hard nor feared for my life as much as I did on that day. Trucks of tomatoes were dumped in the streets, and I soon found myself picking up handfuls of squashed fruit and throwing them at whoever happened to be closest. Most people participating were considerate, but a few were not. I was thankful that I'd left my phone back at the hotel and worn clothes I didn't mind getting ruined. I did wish I'd invested in a pair of goggles though, as being hit in the eye by a tomato meant I couldn't see out of it very well for a couple of days. It was definitely an experience I'll never forget, but one I have no desire to repeat!

B Joe Haythorpe

I went with friends to the mud festival held in Boryeong, South Korea because several of them had been before, loved it and wanted to go again. The two-week event is centred on an area of Boryeong beach set up with water slides and pools to play in while covered in huge quantities of the mineral-rich mud that's taken from the shore near the city. It's great fun for the entire family as well as groups of friends. Apart from playing in the mud, we also attended some great concerts and shopped for mud-based skin creams. Although it's only been going since 1998, it already attracts millions of Koreans and Western tourists annually. But if you're considering going, book your accommodation early as room rates triple closer to the event. All in all, this festival was by far the most fun one I've ever been to.

C Charlie Traynor

Cheese Rolling on Cooper's Hill in Gloucestershire, England is the ideal activity for fans of extreme sports whether as spectators or as participants, and is definitely one of the craziest traditions I've ever witnessed. I watched in amazement as madly courageous men and women threw themselves down a steep hill, tumbling head over heels, while chasing a large round cheese. The cheese always gets to the bottom of the hill first, but for each race there is a prize (a cheese worth a lot of money) for the first person to do so. Thankfully, that day everyone survived without seriously hurting themselves. The event is free, but because of the large crowds, I struggled to find a place from which I could actually see much of the action or use my camera. There were also four uphill races, but they were a lot less exciting.

D Louisa Darke

During the Monkey Buffet Festival in Lopburi, Thailand, cakes, fruit and vegetables are piled up on tables in the streets for 3000 local monkeys to enjoy. The festival was established to boost tourism in the area, and it's worked: huge crowds now travel there from all over the world, many dressed in monkey costumes. There is traditional music, dance and sculpture, all with a monkey theme, and the monkeys themselves roam free. They have no fear of people, and we were warned that they might try to grab our phones, hats or even jewellery and run off with them. I'm glad to say they didn't, but at one point a young monkey jumped up onto my shoulder, making me very uncomfortable. We were given sticks to protect ourselves from the boldest monkeys, but I didn't want to use one. I was glad when the monkey climbed down. However, it was very entertaining to watch the animals from a distance, happily playing and eating.

 Exam facts

- In this part, you read one long text divided into sections or four to six shorter parts.
- There are ten short questions.
- You have to choose the section or shorter text that contains information that matches each of the questions.

© Cambridge University Press and UCLES 2015

Entertainment and media

1 ▶ **Write the end of the second sentences so that they mean the same as the first. Use the word in brackets.**

1. When members of the audience enter the theatre, someone checks their tickets. (have)

   When members of the audience enter the theatre, they ....

2. When stars drive to the hotel, someone drives their car to the car park. (have)

   When stars drive to the hotel, they ....

3. Nearly every time famous people go out, someone takes their photo. (get)

   Nearly every time famous people go out, they ....

4. When authors write a bestseller, someone edits it. (get)

   When authors write a bestseller, they ....

5. Famous people write autobiographies and someone publishes them. (get)

   Famous people write autobiographies and they ....

6. Before actors go on stage someone does their make-up. (have)

   Before actors go on stage they ....

☑ Exam task

2 ▶ **You are going to read an article about what five young people think about fame. For questions 1–10 choose from the people (A–E). The people may be chosen more than once.**

Which person

admits he finds certain aspects of fame attractive?	**1**
believes that fame makes those who get it focus too much on themselves?	**2**
describes some common beliefs about fame that he feels are untrue?	**3**
is critical of the way that famous people are treated?	**4**
says he is uninterested in the details of famous people's lives?	**5**
thinks being famous makes people distrust the motives of people they are close to?	**6**
outlines how fame can benefit society?	**7**
explains why he has some respect for everyone who is famous?	**8**
lists some of the ways that people might attract an audience?	**9**
suggests childhood experiences may cause some people to seek fame?	**10**

Fame and fortune

Five young people say what they think about fame.

A   Stefan

Fame will bring you all the money, attention and love you could ever want! It will solve all your problems and make you feel fantastic! You'll never feel lonely ever again! These are the kind of lies about being famous the media feeds society through various channels. We are taught to highly value public attention, which celebrity-chasing individuals can get by eating insects in online videos, living in a crowded TV house, or being cruel or offensive on social media – it seems how we get it does not matter.

B   Leo

One thing I've noticed about famous people is that they've often been through a negative event during their early lives – like the loss of a parent, or being rejected by a key figure in their lives. This has left them with a lack of self-confidence, which drives them to seek success on stage or screen to give them a sense of self-worth. The problem is that when they achieve fame, they begin to wonder if people love them for who they really are, or simply for the fact that they are famous. This makes it challenging for famous people to form secure relationships. Partly as a result of that, they end up socialising with other celebrities who have similar emotional problems, and this makes their situation worse.

C   Franz

To be honest, the idea of being on a stage and having everyone focus on you is quite appealing to me, but I know that there's no way I'd enjoy the reality of being famous. When everyone knows who you are, it's as if you're not human anymore. Fame means endless requests for pictures, autographs and stories for the tabloid press. Every mistake is exaggerated and nothing in your family life remains private. How could you not get fed up with that? I think that's why some stars become arrogant or unhappy, and unable to act like normal people, especially if they become famous at a young age and have to grow up with the public watching their every move.

D   Mahomet

There is nothing wrong with being famous if it's because you are very skilled at something, whether you've written a bestseller, you're a brilliant surgeon or a great entertainer. Fame based on earning the respect or admiration of your readers, patients or audience can inspire people. It also provides a link between people – common ground that helps us feel part of a community. However, when fame is used merely as self-promotion to gain money or more attention for its own sake, then it adds very little to the world.

E   Johann

I try to avoid reading about so-called 'stars' – they're just people like everyone else, and I really don't care if they're getting married, divorced or buying a new pet cat! On the whole, people who are famous seem to live in another world, where they are the only thing of importance. They are obsessed with their own lives, and the longer they stay in the headlines, the worse they get. One thing I do admire, though, is the ability they all share to recover time after time, when the media turns against them or their latest project has failed.

☑ **Exam tips**

- Read the questions first and underline the most important words.
- The same information in the questions and text is usually written using different words or phrases. Look for words, phrases and sentences in the text that match the question in terms of meaning.
- When you think you have found the answer to a question, read the question and the evidence in the text again carefully.

The environment

1 Make sentences with *It is ...*, a word or phrase from the box and the information below. Sometimes there is more than one possible answer.

claimed	not known	predicted	sometimes	said	thought

1. .... global conservation is fighting a losing battle.
2. .... 11% of animals worldwide will be endangered by 2050.
3. .... how many insect species have already become extinct.
4. .... numbers of farmland birds will continue to rise.
5. .... the word *butterfly* may originate from people calling one species a 'butter-coloured fly'.
6. .... a new species of frog has been discovered in a remote area of jungle.

☑ Exam task

2 You are going to read five paragraphs from the website of a wildlife conservation organisation. For questions 1–10 choose from the paragraphs (A–E). The paragraphs may be chosen more than once.

Which paragraph

points out that some aspects of the volunteers' work is surprisingly challenging?	**1** ☐
includes a promise about the excellence of some services it offers?	**2** ☐
says that the organisation is keen to recruit people who have a certain hobby?	**3** ☐
lists a number of threats to animals that live in the sea?	**4** ☐
mentions the length of time that the organisation has existed?	**5** ☐
outlines the characteristics that are useful for volunteers to have?	**6** ☐
warns that the measures taken to protect one species are not enough?	**7** ☐
mentions features which can help distinguish one animal from another of the same species?	**8** ☐
mentions how the organisation informs the public about its research findings?	**9** ☐
describes the process involved in one kind of information-gathering session?	**10** ☐

The Sea Mammal Institute

A The Sea Mammal Institute is a wildlife conservation organisation set up to protect whales, dolphins and porpoises. Our team of professional researchers work together with volunteers to identify and monitor the numbers and locations of these creatures in order to gain valuable knowledge of the state of our ocean environment, and the impact of climate change, noise disturbance, chemical pollution and overfishing in our seas. We are also proud of the educational role we perform, increasing public knowledge and understanding of sea mammals, and passing on what our data has taught us through community group talks and school visits.

B Our organisation relies heavily on volunteers, who help collect data and then input, organise and analyse it. Volunteers interested in photography are always very welcome to help update our photo-identification catalogue – a collection of pictures of all the different species we monitor – and organise our ever-growing image library. If you would like to be a volunteer, the most straightforward way to get involved is to contact the organisation's co-ordinator in your area, and join him or her for a sea watch. Anyone with enthusiasm and a pair of binoculars can take part – and, as you'll learn if you join us, patience is pretty essential too!

C Although we are pleased to receive any information on public sightings of whales, dolphins and porpoises, it is also important for us to have 'effort-related' data collected by trained volunteers. 'Effort-related' data is that recorded by observers who time their watch and note down specific environmental data every 15 minutes. It doesn't matter how long each watch is, provided that its date and location are carefully noted down along with any details about sightings of sea creatures. We emphasise the need to do some basic training in observation before taking part in a watch because it's not as simple as it sounds. For example, despite the bottlenose dolphin being the probably the best-known type of dolphin, it is in fact rather tricky to identify with any confidence, since it has no clear pattern markings. The upper part of its body is plain dark brown and the underside is a paler brown or grey. So volunteers need plenty of guidance regarding how exactly to recognise it.

D The Sea Mammal Institute has been running courses for over twenty years, making it the most experienced organisation for training observers and students interested in sea animals in the country. It provides staff training for leading conservation organisations, and guarantees a very high quality of training from expert course leaders. The two-day introductory course recommended for new volunteer observers teaches participants the basics of how to identify different species, estimate group size, distinguish between calves, juveniles and adults and to assess the state of the sea. Plenty of practice conducting both land and boat-based surveys is given. Also included are sessions on basic photographic techniques to enable observers to identify an individual animal through distinctive markings, body size or injury scars.

E One of the strengths of our organisation is that we do long-term, continuous research. Over the 25 years since Sea Watch was set up, some significant insights have resulted from this research. For example, our monitoring of bottlenose dolphins shows that even in locations that are already controlled conservation areas, large numbers of motorised boats may be causing changes in their behaviour. Although strict codes of conduct stop boats approaching dolphins too closely or too fast, it is believed that the creatures' social structures are being affected by the presence of so many boats in these areas.

 Get it right!

Look at the sentence below. Then try to correct the mistake.

It is told that animals suffer a lot if they are kept in cages or behind fences.

AN ESSAY

Hobbies and leisure

1 Complete the opinions below using words from the box. Which opinions do you agree with?

believe	in my	personally	say	see	seems	view	would

1.
.... opinion, young people don't get enough free time these days. They're under too much pressure at school.

2.
I .... that having hobbies you enjoy helps you to work hard and do well in exams.

3.
It .... to me that there are lots of opportunities to do exciting hobbies such as rock climbing or skydiving, but you always need money to join in!

4.
In my .... most teenagers spend too much time on their mobile phones. They should get out and spend more time making friends!

5.
As I .... it, the internet has created loads of opportunities to explore new hobbies and interests, such as film-making and photography.

6.
I would .... that schools should do more to encourage young people to have a range of interests in their free time.

7.
Most people .... agree that it isn't healthy to spend all your time working or studying.

8.
.........................., I think it's really important to be active and do sport in your free time.

2

In your English class you have been talking about hobbies and free time. Now your English teacher has asked you to write an essay.

Write your essay using all the notes and giving reasons for your points of view. Write your essay in 140–190 words in an appropriate style.

Young people today spend too much of their free time playing video games. Do you agree?
Notes Write about:
1. things you can learn from video games 2. doing exercise 3. .... (your own idea)

3

Complete the paragraphs about people's hobbies with the correct words and phrases.

I started playing the guitar a year ago, and I would recommend it as a hobby to anyone who likes music. Taking up an instrument doesn't need to be expensive. **(1)** *Therefore / For instance*, you can buy a second-hand guitar very cheaply online. **(2)** *As for / Therefore* lessons, you don't need to pay a teacher because there are lots of videos online that you can use to teach yourself to play. Playing music is really relaxing. **(3)** *Moreover / For example*, there are lots of opportunities to join a band and start performing. **(4)** *To sum up / In this way*, you can improve your skills and make friends. Why not have a go?

I have always been interested in food. **(5)** *For instance / For this reason*, I was delighted when my local college started offering cookery lessons. The classes weren't expensive, and I **(6)** *therefore / in this way* decided to sign up. I loved it from the start, and I've learned to make some great dishes. Cooking is a really creative hobby. **(7)** *As a result / Furthermore*, it's something you can share with your friends, because everyone enjoys eating good food! It isn't expensive, either. **(8)** *As a result / To sum up*, cooking is an affordable, fun and sociable thing to do in your free time – you should definitely try it!

☑ **Exam facts**

- In this part, you are given a question or statement and some notes.
- You have to write an essay of between 140 and 190 words that gives your opinion about the question or statement.
- You have to include the points given in the notes and an idea of your own.

AN ESSAY

Health and fitness

1 ▸ Read the task and the essay. Then read the sentences and choose the correct answer, a or b.

Should adverts for junk food be allowed on TV?

Notes

Write about:
1. the problem with junk food
2. the effect of advertising on children
3. .... (your own idea)

Only £4.99!

1. People see adverts for junk food such as burgers and chocolate bars on their TV screens every day. Although there are problems with people eating too much junk food, banning adverts for it is not necessarily the answer.
2. It is true that eating junk food can have a bad effect on people's health. Eating foods that contain a lot of fat or sugar can make people overweight and cause health problems such as heart attacks. Moreover, advertising can have a very strong effect on children, especially if adverts use popular cartoon characters. This can encourage them to develop unhealthy eating habits.
3. On the other hand, eating junk food from time to time is not bad for your health, and can be nice on special occasions. Imagine a day at the seaside without an ice cream, or a birthday celebration without a box of chocolates! Without advertising, people wouldn't have good choices for these products.
4. In my view, the most important thing is to educate children about the importance of a healthy diet. In this way, they can enjoy junk foods occasionally, but also stay fit and healthy.

1. The first sentence of the essay ...

    a introduces the topic and gives the writer's opinion.

    b gives a general introduction to the topic.

2. In paragraph 1, the writer ...

    a contrasts two different opinions about junk food and advertising.

    b gives two similar opinions about the problem with junk food.

3. Paragraph 1 is ...

    a quite short.

    b longer than all the other paragraphs.

4. In paragraph 2, the writer ...

    a gives arguments for and against junk foods.

    b gives detailed arguments about the problem with junk foods.

5. In paragraph 3, the writer ...

    a adds more arguments against junk food.

    b gives a different point of view about junk food.

6. Paragraph 4 ...

   a states the writer's conclusion and opinion.

   b repeats all the opinions from paragraphs 2 and 3.

☑ Exam task

In your English class you have been talking about healthy living. Now your English teacher has asked you to write an essay.

Write your essay using all the notes and giving reasons for your points of view. Write your essay in 140–190 words in an appropriate style.

Schools are responsible for teaching young people all the skills they need to stay fit and healthy. Do you agree?
Notes Write about:
1. exercise 2. food 3. .... (your own idea)

3

Complete the sentences with the correct words and phrases.

1. *Although / However* Jack is only fifteen, he takes his health very seriously.
2. Junk food is cheap, *despite / whereas* healthy foods are often quite expensive.
3. Schools can't force young people to do exercise. *On the other hand / Whereas*, they can certainly encourage them to take up a sport.
4. Joining a gym is quite expensive. *Although / However*, it can bring a lot of benefits.
5. I went for a run this morning *despite / in spite* the bad weather.
6. *While / Nevertheless* a lot of people would like to cycle to work, they don't do it because they think the roads are not safe.
7. We all know that junk food is bad for us, but *in spite of / although* this, we all eat it from time to time.
8. Walking is a very gentle form of exercise. *Nevertheless / Although*, it is still very good for your health.

☑ Exam tips

- Quickly plan what you are going to include in your essay.
- Remember to include a brief introduction and a conclusion.
- Make sure you answer the question, include all the points given in the notes, including your own idea, and give reasons for your opinions.

AN ESSAY

The environment

1 Match the definitions with the words and phrases.

1. This gas causes pollution, and is causing the earth to become hotter.	**a** drought
2. This is a clean form of energy that uses light from the sun.	**b** carbon dioxide
3. This happens when there is a lot of rain.	**c** climate change
4. This describes animals that could disappear in the future.	**d** famine
5. The process of taking action to protect the environment.	**e** flooding
6. This is the process in which the weather is gradually changing because of pollution.	**f** endangered
7. This is a situation in which a lot of people suffer because they have no food.	**g** conservation
8. This happens when the land becomes very dry because there is no rain.	**h** reserve
9. To make water, air, soil, etc. dirty or harmful.	**i** pollute
10. This is an area of land where animals and plants are protected.	**j** solar

2 Read the task and the main paragraphs of the essay. Then read concluding paragraphs a–c and answer the questions. Which is the best concluding paragraph? Why?

Individuals can do a lot to help the environment. Do you agree?

> **Notes**
> Write about:
> 1. recycling
> 2. transport
> 3. .... (your own idea)

The environment is a very important problem in the world today. While governments clearly need to take action to protect the world we live in, individuals can also make a big contribution to improving the environment.

Firstly, people can buy products that can be recycled. When we throw things away, they often end up in the environment and cause a lot of pollution. If everyone recycled as much as possible, there would be a lot less rubbish in our seas and under the ground.

Secondly, people can think about how they travel to school or work. Cars have a very bad effect on the environment, so individuals can help by walking or cycling, or using public transport.

However, individuals cannot solve all our environmental problems. There are some things that only governments can do, such as deciding which forms of energy the country should invest in, or deciding whether to build new airports.

a   *Another thing that individuals can do is refuse to fly, as planes cause a lot of pollution. On the other hand, it is the government's responsibility to decide on the price of flying. If they put the prices up, this would prevent people from using this damaging form of transport.*

b   *Both individuals and governments can play an important role in protecting the environment, and both should take this problem seriously and do what they can to help. If this happens, I believe that in the future the world will be a cleaner and safer place to live in.*

c   *Individuals can make a big difference to the environment by choosing environmentally friendly forms of transport, and by reusing or recycling products. However, governments must also help protect our world, for example by choosing clean forms of energy. Scientists all agree that we must take action soon.*

Which concluding paragraph …

1. introduces a new argument?

2. repeats all the arguments from the previous paragraphs?

3. provides a short summary of the arguments from the previous paragraphs?

4. expresses two different points of view? (2 answers)

5. ends with the writer's opinion?

6. ends by expressing someone else's opinion?

 Exam task

3

In your English class you have been talking about the environment. Now your English teacher has asked you to write an essay.

Write your essay using all the notes and giving reasons for your points of view. Write your essay in 140–190 words in an appropriate style.

There are lots of things governments could do to help deal with environmental problems. Do you agree?

Notes

Write about:

1. pollution

2. cost

3. .... (your own idea)

Get it right!

Look at the sentence below. Then try to correct the mistake.

Concluding, I think life nowadays is better than it was in the past.

AN ARTICLE

☑ **Exam facts**

- In this part, you choose one writing task from four options.
- In **Cambridge English: First** the possible tasks are: an article, an informal letter or email, a formal letter or email, a review and a report.
- In **Cambridge English: First for Schools** the possible tasks are: an article, an informal letter or email, a formal letter or email, a review and a story.
- You have to write between 140 and 190 words.

Travel and holidays

1 **Complete the travel problems with the words and phrases in the boxes. There are two words in each box that you don't need.**

horn	lane	overtake	reverse	rush hour	traffic jam

Driving in Paris isn't easy. We made the mistake of trying to drive across the city at 7.30 in the morning – right in the middle of the morning **(1)** .... ! First, we were stuck in a huge **(2)** .... for about twenty minutes. When we started moving again, we tried to **(3)** .... another car because it was going so slowly, but we ended up in the wrong **(4)** .... by mistake and had to turn off in completely the wrong direction – it was a nightmare!

♡ 12   💬 3

connection	immigration	landing	scheduled	stopover	terminal

I flew to Australia last summer with my family and it was awful! We chose a cheap route, changing at Singapore. Although our flight from London to Singapore was **(5)** .... to leave at 6.30 in the morning, it didn't take off until 10.30, so we spent hours waiting in the **(6)** .... Then, because this flight was delayed, we missed our **(7)** .... to Sydney, so we had to spend an extra day in Singapore. When we finally got on our plane to Australia, the weather was really bad, and the **(8)** .... at Sydney airport was very scary. I was so glad to finally be there!

♡ 7   💬 1

2 Choose the correct alternatives to complete the article.

A trip to a different world

Are you looking for somewhere different to go on holiday? Why not try India? I went there last year, and had an amazing three weeks!

(1) *As soon as / At first* we drove out of the airport, I felt as though I was in a different world. There were so many people, and so many interesting things to look at. I couldn't speak **(2)** *after / for some time* because I was so busy looking around me. Half an hour **(3)** *later / longer* we arrived at our hotel, left our bags there and decided to go out and explore. **(4)** *Immediately / At first*, everything felt strange. Seeing cows on the streets of busy towns and cities was certainly new to me! But **(5)** *before long / at the same time* I started to feel more at home in this fascinating and colourful country. We saw many wonderful sights **(6)** *as / between* we travelled around. One day we watched some people riding camels through a town centre, while **(7)** *finally / at the same time* normal life went on around them! Everyone we met was really friendly. I felt ill one day when we were out sightseeing, and people **(8)** *at first / immediately* came to offer me help. When it was **(9)** *lastly / finally* time for us to go home, I was surprised at how upset I felt. I can't wait to go back!

☑ Exam task

3 You see this announcement on an English-language website. Write your answer in 140–190 words in an appropriate style.

Articles wanted

The best holiday I have ever had

Where was your best holiday, and who were you with?
What did you do, and why was it so good?

We will publish the best articles on our website.

Write your **article**.

AN INFORMAL LETTER OR EMAIL

Cultures and customs

1   **Complete the travel advice with the words and phrases in the box. Which two people offer help?**

> could always   good idea   how about   If I were you   if you like   must   recommend
> why don't   worth   would you like

● ● ●   ⟳ 🔍 🏠

**I love travelling, and I love going to festivals.
What are the best festivals in the world to see?**

I'd definitely **(1)** .... the carnival in Rio de Janeiro, in Brazil. I can help you find a place to stay, **(2)** ....
Fabio

If you're in Thailand in April, it's **(3)** .... joining in with the Songkran celebrations. Our New Year begins on 13 April, and we celebrate by having big water fights in the street! You'll get wet, but it's great fun. **(4)** .... , I'd wear old clothes, though!
Alak

(5) .... you come to Pamplona, in Spain? In July each year, we have the 'Running of the bulls' festival, when bulls run through the streets and some (crazy!) people run with them! **(6)** .... me to send you a link to the website?
Ana

You really **(7)** .... see the St Patrick's Day Parade in Boston. It's on March 17, and some of the costumes are amazing! It's a **(8)** .... to get there early, so you get a good view of the parade!
Emma

(9) .... coming to Scotland for Hogmanay? That's our name for New Year's Eve. There are brilliant fireworks in Edinburgh at midnight, and you **(10)** .... travel a bit further north and go skiing afterwards if you want!
Fergus

2 Read the two emails below. Then answer the questions.

> **From:** Tom
> **Subject:** Summer holidays
>
> Hello Sam,
>
> How are things? Do you fancy coming to stay with me for a few days in the summer holidays? My uncle's given me his old canoe, so we could try it out on the lake near our house. Do you think we'll be able to steer it together? Plus, I've got a new tent, so we could camp out if the weather's good. Should be fun! Let me know.
>
> Write soon,
> Tom

> **From:** Sam
> **Subject:** Summer holidays
>
> Hi Tom,
>
> Great to hear from you! Yeah, that sounds amazing! I've done canoeing before, so I reckon we'll be fine. Camping sounds pretty cool too!
>
> See you soon,
> Sam

Find ...

1. two ways of beginning informal emails. ....
2. two ways of ending informal emails. ....
3. four contracted forms. ....
4. an informal way of giving an opinion. ....
5. an informal word for *also*. ....
6. an informal way of inviting someone to do something. ....
7. an example of a word omitted from a sentence to make it more informal. ....
8. an informal word for *very*. ....

☑ *Exam task*

3 **You have received an email from your English-speaking pen friend Rob. Write your answer in 140–190 words in an appropriate style.**

> **From:** Rob
> **Subject:** Festivals
>
> Can you help me with a class project? I have to write about festivals in different countries, and the way people celebrate them. Can you tell me about your favourite festival in your country? What is it and when does it take place? How do people usually celebrate it? Why do you enjoy it?
> Thanks,
> Rob

Write your **email**.

☑ *Exam tips*

- You must answer all the questions in the letter. You may need to give advice, offer help, make suggestions or express your opinions.
- Remember to use informal language.
- Don't forget to open your letter or email correctly (*Hi Alison, Dear Nick*) and include an appropriate closing (*Best wishes, All the best*).

A FORMAL LETTER OR EMAIL

Education and work

1 Complete the sentences with the words in the box. Which TWO sentences are false?

academic	campus	graduate	institution	lecturer	qualify	seminar	sit

1. You go to university to get .... qualifications.
2. Cambridge University is a well-known educational ....
3. A .... is a discussion class for a small group of students.
4. A .... is an area where there are university buildings and accommodation for students.
5. Most students .... and are awarded their degree after three years of study.
6. In Britain, it takes around four years of study to .... as doctor.
7. Most university students .... exams at the end of each year of their course.
8. A .... is a university teacher who usually teaches small groups of students.

☑ *Exam task*

2 Read the task. Write your answer in 140–190 words in an appropriate style.
You have seen this advertisement for a summer job.

> **Young people wanted**
>
> We are looking for enthusiastic, outgoing young people to work as team leaders in our summer camps, organising activities for children aged 7–12. You must get on well with children and be good at sport.
>
> Please apply saying why you are suitable for the job and what qualifications and experience you have that would be useful in the job.

Write your **letter of application**.

3a Choose the correct relative pronouns to complete the sentences. Then answer the questions.

1. I have found a course *which / who / when* I would like to apply for.
2. York University, *which / where / when* I studied, is one of the best universities in the country.
3. Rob has run his own business since 2012, *where / when / which* he left university.
4. I get on well with the tutors *which / who / whose* teach the course.
5. Tim, *who / whose / which* parents are both teachers, always works hard at school.
6. I asked my uncle about the university *which / where / when* he studied.
7. Travelling is the part of my job *where / which / who* I love the most.
8. Janet, *who / where / which* I work with, has got a degree in medicine.

    a. Which sentences are defining relative clauses, and which are non-defining?

    ....

    b. In which sentences could you omit the relative pronoun?

    ....

    c. In which sentences could you also use the relative pronoun that?

    ....

3b Complete the sentences with the correct relative pronoun. If no relative pronoun is needed, write ' – '.

1. My brother studied at the University of Cambridge, ... is one of the most prestigious universities in the world.
2. In the UK, a 'fresher' is a student .... has recently started college or university.
3. What was the name of that book by Emily Brontë .... we read in our English literature class last year?
4. Will, ... dream is to be a graphic designer, built our new school website – it looks amazing!
5. May is the month .... university students normally sit their exams.
6. Can you see that really tall building over there? That's .... my sister works.
7. My grandmother, ... was the first person in my family to go to university, is probably the most intelligent person I know.
8. A careers adviser is a person .... you can talk to if you aren't sure what job you'd like to do in the future.

☑ *Exam tips*

- Remember to divide your letter into paragraphs.
- Make sure you use formal language.
- You must open your letter or email correctly (*Dear Mr Anderson, Dear Madam*) and include an appropriate closing (*Yours sincerely, Yours faithfully*).

A REVIEW

Shopping and fashion

1 Complete the fashion show reviews with the adjectives in the boxes.

dreadful	fantastic	impressive

I loved Kurt Jackson's last collection, and this one is even better – some of his dress designs are absolutely
(1) .... ! Look out for his stunning evening dresses! He isn't so good at menswear, though, and some of his suits were really **(2)** .... Overall, though, this is a very **(3)** .... collection from such a young designer!

bizarre	delightful	genuine

Poppy Grey is known for her slightly strange designs, but some of her latest clothes look really
(4) .... and are definitely not things you would want to wear! The only piece I liked was a
(5) .... pink summer dress, which I would love to buy if I could afford it! I think Poppy has some
(6) .... talent, but she should definitely stick to more traditional designs.

brilliant	entertaining	poor

This is Joe Darnley's first big collection, and he used a lot of clever tricks to make the show lively and **(7)** .... However, I think his basic designs are
(8) .... and lacking in imagination. This wasn't a **(9)** .... start to his designing career, and he will need to improve if he wants to reach the top!

2

Read the task. Write your answer in 140–190 words in an appropriate style.

Reviews wanted

We are looking for reviews of online clothes shops. Write a review of an online clothes shop you have used recently. Explain what kinds of clothes it sells, how the prices compare to other shops and how easy it is to find what you want. Would you recommend this online shop to other people?

The best reviews will be published in next month's magazine.

Write your **review**.

3 Choose the correct alternative to complete the recommendations.

1. I *would / must* recommend this book to anyone who likes crime fiction.

5. I wouldn't *recommend / advise* this shop to people who have only a limited budget.

6. If you like fashionable clothes, you should *completely / definitely* check out this new website.

2. I'd *suggest / advise* against paying too much for a tablet, when technology is changing so fast.

7. I *thoroughly / incredibly* recommend this restaurant to all lovers of good food.

3. The new shopping centre is definitely worth *a visit / to visit*.

4. I would suggest *to shop around / shopping around* before you buy a new camera – there are some great deals online.

8. Her fashion shows are very popular, so I would advise *you to buy / that you buy* a ticket well in advance.

☑ **Exam tips**

- You should describe the thing or place you are reviewing. Try to use a range of descriptive adjectives and adverbs.
- Remember to include your opinions and give reasons – say why you liked it or why you didn't.
- You usually need to say if you'd recommend the subject of your review to other people or not.

A REPORT

 Exam fact

If you're taking **Cambridge English: First**, in Writing Part 2, there may be a question asking you to write a report. You won't be asked to write a report if you're taking *Cambridge English: First for Schools*.

Places and buildings

> **A REPORT** is usually written for a superior (e.g. a teacher) or a peer group (e.g. members of an English club). Candidates are expected to give some factual information and make suggestions or recommendations. A report should be clearly organised and may include headings.

1a **Complete the sentences with the correct form of the verbs in brackets. Sometimes more than one form is possible.**

1. We .... posters to advertise the new swimming pool. (put up)
2. New bus shelters could .... near the sports centre. (provide)
3. It would be beneficial .... better public transport in the town. (have)
4. If there were studios available, young artists .... to develop their talents. (be able)
5. We recommend that the old cinema should .... (pull down)
6. Our main recommendation is .... the old bank into a youth cafe. (turn)
7. We would suggest .... a new arts centre. (open)
8. The museum needs to .... so that more people will visit it. (improve)

1b **Complete the sentences with your own ideas.**

1. To help protect the environment you should ....
....
2. In order to improve public transport in my town or city, my main recommendation
   would be ....
3. I would recommend that visitors to my town or city ....
....
4. In my place of study or work, it would be beneficial..
....
5. In order to improve the main shopping area of my town or city I suggest ....
....
6. To improve leisure facilities in my town or city I would suggest ....
....

2 **Read the task. Write your answer in 140–190 words in an appropriate style.**

> Your local government wants to improve leisure facilities in your town. Your English teacher wants to know the opinions of the students at your language school.
> Write a report for your teacher, explaining what facilities there are already in your town and recommending new facilities that would benefit young people.

Write your **report**.

3 **Rewrite the sentences with the correct punctuation.**

1. the new sports centre opened in june

   ....

2. what facilities are available

   ....

3. thats terrible news

   ....

4. im going to the gym she said

   ....

5. the most popular sports are football tennis and rugby

   ....

6. if they opened a new cinema a lot of people would go to it

   ....

7. although there is a youth club not many people use it

   ....

8. finally i would recommend building a new swimming pool

   ....

- In the first paragraph, you should say what the purpose of your report is – why you are writing it.
- Make sure you organise your report into paragraphs. You can include section headings to make the structure clearer.
- Remember to write in full sentences and use a range of language with accurate spelling.

A STORY

☑ **Exam fact**

If you're taking **Cambridge English: First for Schools**, in Writing Part 2, there may be a question asking you to write a story. You won't be asked to write a story if you're taking *Cambridge English: First*.

Family and friends

1 **Complete the story with the correct form of the verbs in brackets. Use the past simple, past continuous or past perfect.**

Ellie rang the doorbell and **(1)** .... (stand) by the door while she **(2)** .... (wait) for her friend to answer it. She was feeling slightly nervous. Her friend, Sara, **(3)** .... (call) her earlier to ask her to come round at six o'clock, but she **(4)** .... (not give) her a reason. Ellie **(5)** .... (not know) what to expect.

Before long, Sara **(6)** .... (come) to the door. "Come in," she **(7)** .... (say) cheerfully. "We'll go into the living room." "Why are there no lights on?" Ellie **(8)** .... (ask). "Oh, I **(9)** .... (watch) a film," Ellie replied casually. "I like watching films in the dark. I'll put the lights on now." As soon as she put the lights on, Ellie realised why Sara **(10)** .... (be) so secretive earlier. The room was full of all her friends, and one of them **(11)** .... (hold) a cake with candles on it. "Happy birthday!" they all **(12)** .... (shout) !

☑ **Exam task**

2 **Read the task. Write your answer in 140–190 words in an appropriate style.**

Send us a story!

We are looking for stories for our English-language magazine for young people. Your story must **begin** with this sentence:

When Max opened the letter, he was so excited that that he started dancing around the room.

Your story must include:

- a journey
- a meeting

Write your **story**.

3 Read the speech bubbles. Then complete the sentences with adverbs formed from the adjectives in the box.

cheerful confident furious honest impatient nervous proud unexpected

1. Where is she? It's so annoying! I can't believe she's so late!

Fran was waiting .... for her friend.

2. Of course I'm very angry – you've broken my phone!

Sam reacted .... when his brother broke his phone.

3. What a great day for going to the beach!

Johnny greeted his friends .... as they got on the bus.

4. Of course I can do it! No problem!

Ralph accepted the challenge ....

5. I won the tournament! I'm so pleased with myself!

Dan told his parents .... that he had won the tournament.

6. What are you doing here, Freddie? I thought you were on holiday.

Freddie arrived ....

7. Yes, I promise I'll tell you the truth about what happened.

Mia promised to speak .... about what had happened.

8. I'm really worried that I may have failed my exams!

Ruth opened her exam results ....

☑ *Exam tips*

- You must begin your story with the prompt sentence.
- Make sure you include both the ideas mentioned in the instructions.
- Remember to use a range of past tenses – past simple, past continuous and past perfect.

Education and study

1 Put the words in order to make *yes / no* questions. Write the short answer. Then write another sentence to explain your answer.

1. education / you / at / are / in / moment / the / ?

....

....

2. favourite / you / teacher / did / have / school / a / at / ?

....

....

3. there / to / like / subject / more / know / is / a / about / you'd / ?

....

....

4. challenging / have / a / found / ever / you / subject / ?

....

....

5. two / can / speak / languages / more / you / than / ?

....

....

6. in / taught / creative / schools / like / should / art / be / subjects / ?

....

....

7. to / subjects / could / different / would / if / you / choose / you / study / ?

....

....

8. enjoy / maths / learning / science / you / do / about / and / ?

....

....

2 Match adjectives 1–8 with their synonyms a–h.

1. fascinated	**a** nervous
2. unsure	**b** motivated
3. anxious	**c** doubtful
4. worried	**d** eager
5. furious	**e** annoyed
6. enthusiastic	**f** concerned
7. optimistic	**g** positive
8. inspired	**h** interested

☑ Exam task

🔊 **Track 1** You will hear people talking in eight different situations. For questions 1–8, choose the best answer (A, B or C).

1. You hear a woman telling her son about her favourite schoolteacher.

   What did the woman like about her history teacher?

   A his acting skills

   B his sense of humour

   C his passion for the subject

2. You hear a girl talking about maths.

   What does the girl enjoy most about maths?

   A getting clear answers

   B applying it to everyday life

   C solving difficult questions

3. You hear a man telling a friend about being unable to study art at school.

   He says that he would have liked to study art in order to

   A know more about art history.

   B learn some techniques.

   C follow a career in art.

4. You hear two students discussing a sports class they have just attended.

   What do they agree on about the class?

   A how relevant the information was for them

   B how knowledgeable the teacher was

   C how inspiring the new ideas were

5. You hear a girl telling a friend about her brother.

   How does the girl's brother feel about starting university?

   A anxious about meeting new people

   B worried about managing the workload

   C concerned about his abilities in his subject

6. You hear a student talking to his teacher about an assignment.

   The boy says that he feels

   A uneasy about having to write about an unfamiliar topic.

   B unsure about how to carry out some research.

   C doubtful about which writing style to use.

7. You hear a science teacher talking to her class.

   What is she doing?

   A cancelling an activity / a plan

   B changing an arrangement

   C correcting some information

8. You hear two friends discussing learning foreign languages.

   They both hold the opinion that

   A communication does not rely on speaking a language.

   B it's possible to learn about culture through language.

   C learning languages is essential for travel.

☑ Exam facts

- In this part, you listen to eight short recordings of one or two people speaking.
- There is a multiple-choice question for each recording.
- You have to choose the correct answer (A, B or C) for the questions.

Hobbies and leisure

1 **Choose the correct form of the adjective to complete the sentences.**

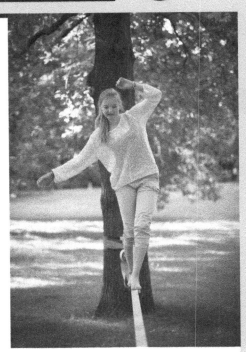

1. How people can walk along a tightrope I'll never know – it's *astonishing / astonished*.
2. I've just started climbing. I've always found it *fascinating / fascinated* to watch.
3. Watching the ice-skaters on the pond kept me *entertaining / entertained* for a couple of hours.
4. I've been trying to finish this puzzle for ages – I can't do it and it's *so irritating / irritated*!
5. Ben was *exhausting / exhausted* when he got back from playing football. He slept for an hour.
6. What a brilliant programme. I feel really *motivating / motivated* to take up a new hobby.
7. Have you seen that new action film? It's *thrilling / thrilled*!
8. I found my new piano teacher very *encouraging / encouraged*. I feel much better about my playing.

2 **Complete the sentences with appropriate question tags.**

1. You go swimming a lot, ... you?
2. You'll come with me to the theatre, ... you?
3. You've done some interesting things, ... you?
4. You're going surfing this weekend, ... you?

3 **Complete 1–4 with appropriate question words. Then answer the questions.**

1. .... 's your favourite band?
....
2. .... kind of films do you like?
....
3. .... would be your perfect weekend?
....
4. .... do you spend your free time?
....

4 🔊 **Track 2 You will hear people talking in eight different situations. For questions 1–8, choose the best answer (A, B or C).**

1. You hear an announcement about a band called the Big Bang.

   What is the purpose of the announcement?

   A to offer music lessons

   B to promote a concert

   C to recruit band members

2. You hear a young woman telling her friend about an article she has read.

   After reading it, the woman says that she felt

   A convinced to try a new activity.

   B encouraged to continue doing an activity.

   C keen to avoid one particular activity.

3. You hear two friends discussing free time.

   They agree that it is important to

   A spend time outside the house.

   B do nothing sometimes.

   C try out a range of activities.

4. You hear a boy telling a friend about the sport of diving.

   What does he say about it?

   A Jumping from the highest board is frightening.

   B Completing a successful dive is motivating.

   C Watching professionals dive is thrilling.

5. You hear two friends talking about hiking.

   What is the man's primary reason for trying it?

   A to see more of where he lives

   B to be physically fitter

   C to overcome a fear

6. You hear a man telling a friend about producing furniture as a hobby.

   Why does the man enjoy working with wood?

   A He takes pleasure in producing something useful.

   B He likes recycling existing pieces of furniture.

   C He appreciates the opportunity to be creative.

7. You hear a review of a film.

   What is the reviewer's opinion of it?

   A the ending was disappointing

   B the scenery was breathtaking

   C the acting was unconvincing

8. You hear two friends talking about taking photos to put on social media websites.

   What does the boy say he likes about it?

   A trying different techniques

   B receiving positive comments

   C analysing his friends' photos

✓ **Exam tips**

- Each question has two sentences. The first sentence tells you who'll be talking and what they'll be talking about; the second sentence is the question you have to answer.
- You'll hear each recording twice. Try to answer the questions the first time you listen, and check your answers the second time you listen.
- If you still don't know the answer after the second listening, make a guess. You won't lose marks for incorrect answers.

Health and fitness

1a Read 1–4 and match with the correct response, a–d.

1. I try my best to eat well and get plenty of rest.	**a** So have I.
2. I can't run very far without getting out of breath.	**b** Nor do I.
3. I don't think you should exercise immediately after eating.	**c** So do I.
4. I've just made a healthy eating and exercise plan.	**d** Neither can I.

1b Now write four sentences about health and fitness to give B's responses.

1. **A:** .... **B:** So can I.
2. **A:** .... **B:** Nor have I.
3. **A:** .... **B:** Neither do I.
4. **A:** .... **B:** Nor can I.

2 Match definitions 1–8 with phrases from the box.

break a record	burn out	do someone good	get out of breath
keep in shape	push yourself	warm up	work out

1. become very tired from doing too much ....
2. make yourself work very hard to achieve something ....
3. do something better than anyone else ....
4. get ready by exercising gently ....
5. be breathing quickly because of doing exercise ....
6. do exercise in order to improve strength ....
7. stay healthy and physically strong ....
8. have a positive effect on someone ....

☑ *Exam task*

🔊 **Track 3 You will hear people talking in eight different situations. For questions 1–8, choose the best answer (A, B or C).**

1. You hear a teacher talking to her class.
   What is she doing?
   A explaining the results of a competition
   B thanking them for taking part in an event
   C encouraging them to complete a challenge

2. You hear two friends talking about learning to ski.
   What do they agree about?
   A how much fun the classes are
   B how difficult it is to learn the techniques
   C how physically tiring the activities can be

3. You hear a sports instructor talking to an athletics class.
   What does he say about the current long jump record?
   A It hasn't been broken for a long time.
   B It will be difficult to break.
   C It's something he has tried to break himself.

4. You hear a girl telling a friend about lessons on eating and exercising that she has done at school.
   How does she feel about what she has learned?
   A doubtful that some of the advice will benefit her
   B surprised by some of the information
   C keen to try out a suggestion

5. You hear a student talking to his sports teacher about getting fit.
   What would the boy like to do?
   A take part in a competitive sport
   B use some gym equipment
   C find a training partner

6. You hear two friends talking about a TV programme they have watched.
   What does the woman think about it?
   A It contained some useful tips.
   B It raised surprising arguments.
   C It discussed interesting new research.

7. You hear an expert talking about what being healthy really means.
   She believes that many people have a mistaken idea about
   A how important social contact is.
   B how much exercise they need.
   C how important it is to have a good diet.

8. You hear a fitness expert talking about warming up before exercise.
   He says that people don't always warm up because they
   A have not been educated about its importance.
   B want their exercise sessions to be quick.
   C don't enjoy preparation exercises.

◉ *Get it right!*

Look at the sentences below. Then try to correct the mistake.

I know you don't like sports. So do I.

Food and drink

1 Put the words into the correct column in the table. Some words fit in more than one column.

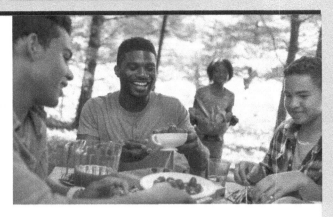

balanced	catering	chop	consume
portion	swallow	taste	vitamin

Noun	Verb	Adjective
....	....	....
....	....	....
....	....	....
....	....	....
....	....	....

☑ Exam task

2 🔊 Track 4 You will hear a girl called Lydia giving a talk about a project she has been involved in on healthy eating. For questions 1–10, complete the sentences with a word or short phrase.

The healthy eating project

Lydia says an alternative name for healthy eating is having a **(1)** ....

Lydia compares the food we eat to **(2)** .... for our bodies.

Lydia says people do not need to avoid certain foods such as **(3)** ....

Lydia says the food pyramid describes the foods we ought to eat and their **(4)** ....

Lydia offers to provide listeners with **(5)** .... which contain fruit and vegetables.

Lydia points out that **(6)** .... is a non-food source of one vitamin.

Lydia says that **(7)** .... is an example of a snack we needn't avoid.

Lydia says the action of **(8)** .... salad items doesn't burn more energy than the food provides.

Lydia gives the example of **(9)** .... as a drink that is useful for our bodies.

Lydia explains that some people think **(10)** .... is a substitute for eating healthily.

3a Match the items from each column to make four definitions.

1.	to cut	up		means to finish everything you've been given
2.	to eat	down		means to eat only a particular food
3.	to heat	on		means to eat or drink less of something
4.	to live	up		means to make warm

3b Write four sentences using each of the phrasal verbs in exercise 3a.

1. ....

2. ....

3. ....

4. ....

4 In pairs, ask and answer the following questions.

1. Do you think you have a healthy diet?

2. In what ways could you eat more healthily?

3. In general do people in your country eat more healthily now than they used to?

4. In which country do you think people have the healthiest diet? And the worst?

☑ **Exam facts**

- In this part, you listen to a recording of one person speaking.
- There are ten sentences with some information missing.
- You have to write words from the recording to complete the sentences.

© Cambridge University Press and UCLES 2015

Work

1 Put the words into the correct column in the table.

duty	earnings	hire	income	position	profession	take on	task

Responsibility	Salary	Job	Employ
....	....	....	....
....	....	....	....

☑ Exam task

2 🔊 Track 5 You will hear a young woman called Jenny Smythe talking about her job as an events organiser. For questions 1–10, complete the sentences with a word or short phrase.

Jenny Smythe: Events organiser

The events Jenny prefers to organise are **(1)** ....

Jenny is currently organising a street fair in the **(2)** .... quarter of her town.

Jenny feels **(3)** .... about the event she's currently organising.

When Jenny takes on a job, she makes something she calls a '**(4)** ....'.

After talking to clients, Jenny then contacts **(5)** .... , who offer the necessary services.

Jenny uses the word '**(6)** ....' to describe how she feels when an event goes well.

Jenny studied **(7)** .... before she became an events organiser.

Jenny believes that being **(8)** .... is the most important requirement for her job.

When Jenny had a problem with one event, she used the **(9)** .... she had made.

Jenny recommends getting experience in any kind of **(10)** .... job, like the one she did.

3a Choose the appropriate linking word from the box to complete the sentences. Use each linking word once only.

considering	if	now	once	provided	though	where	whereas

1. Olivia did well to get the job .... her lack of experience.
2. I can drive to work .... that I've bought my first car.
3. Ben should do well at work .... that he works hard.
4. I'd like to have a creative job .... I'm not sure what exactly!
5. My sister's got a part-time job .... I work full time.
6. I'll be able to save for a holiday .... I've got a job.
7. Matt's reached the stage in his career .... he'd like to be promoted.
8. I wouldn't have accepted the job .... I'd known how difficult it was.

3b Choose the correct linking word to complete the sentences.

1. My parents have reached the stage in life *where / whereas / now* they need to start planning their retirement.
2. You could become a doctor one day, *once / provided / if* that you study hard and get good grades.
3. *Considering / Provided / Whereas* he never pays attention in class, Dan did surprisingly well in his exams.
4. *Where / Though / Now* I've finished university, I need to start looking for a job.
5. My dad works from home, *where / whereas / considering* my mum's office is in the city.
6. I'll be able to move out of my parents' house *if / though / once* I've found a job.
7. The company wouldn't have hired Sam *whereas / though / if* they'd known how lazy he was.
8. Marta's been working at the same company for 15 years, *though / provided / considering* she really dislikes her job.

> ☑ **Exam tips**
>
> - Before the recording starts, quickly read the instructions, title and ten sentences. Think about what kind of word you need to write in each gap.
> - The ten sentences follow the order of the information in the recording.
> - You usually have to write between one and three words in each gap. You should write the words exactly as you hear them in the recording.

The natural world

1 Complete the sentences with the words from the box.

| climate change | conservation | ecology | endangered |
| evolution | green | pollute | worldwide |

1. .... is another way to say environmentally friendly.

2. .... is the protection of nature.

3. .... means existing or happening all around the Earth.

4. .... is the way the Earth's weather is changing.

5. .... means an animal may disappear forever because there are very few left.

6. .... means to make water, air or soil dirty or harmful.

7. .... is the way in which living things change and develop over millions of years.

8. .... is the relationship between living creatures and their environment, or the scientific study of this.

2 Complete the sentences with the words in brackets. Use the present perfect simple or present perfect continuous.

1. How long .... (you / interested in) animal conservation?

2. I'm dirty because I .... (clear) rubbish from the pond all morning.

3. The study of climate change .... (go on) since the 1800s and continues today.

4. We .... (learn) a lot about evolution so far this term.

5. I .... (just / find out) what being 'green' means.

6. .... (you / ever / look) at the list of endangered animals in our country?

7. My uncle .... (travel) worldwide in search of rare species during his lifetime.

8. We .... (study) ecological disasters in our geography class.

3

🔊 Track 6 You will hear a boy called Jake Castle giving a class presentation about an animal called a hedgehog. For questions 1–10, complete the sentences with a word or short phrase.

Hedgehog conservation

Jake says the hedgehog population is declining as quickly as that of the
(1) ....

Jake says hedgehogs are decreasing in number with the disappearance of
(2) .... and countryside.

Jake explains that hedgehogs particularly like eating worms, along with
(3) ....
and other small creatures.

Jake's club is encouraging people to help make what's known as a 'hedgehog
(4) .... '.

Jake says hedgehogs can pass between gardens through fences or via a
(5) .... which neighbours create.

Jake advises against removing **(6)** .... from a garden, as they can be used to shelter hedgehogs.

Jake hadn't realised that hedgehogs have good **(7)** ....

If a sick hedgehog is found, Jake says the best place to take it is a local
(8) ....

Jake suggests leaving out food which is suitable for **(9)** .... for hedgehogs in winter.

Jake says that the **(10)** .... is a good organisation for those interested in other species.

 Get it right!

Look at the sentence below. Then try to correct the mistake.

Since the end of the Second World War, the world's population is increasing rapidly.

Shopping and fashion

1a **Match 1–8 with a–h to make shopping and fashion phrases.**

1. casually		**a** purchase	
2. designer		**b** dressed	
3. browse		**c** new range	
4. find a		**d** bargain	
5. be		**e** card	
6. make a		**f** the internet	
7. launch a		**g** out of stock	
8. debit		**h** clothing	

1b **Match the phrases from exercise 1a with the definitions.**

1. buy something ....
2. a plastic card used to pay for things directly from your bank account ....
3. expensive clothes made by a well-known company ....
4. find something on sale for less than its true value ....
5. wearing clothes that are not formal ....
6. be unavailable in a shop ....
7. look at information on the web ....
8. start selling a new group of products ....

2 🔊 Track 7 You will hear five short extracts in which people are talking about shopping for clothes. For questions 1–5, choose from the list (A–H), what each speaker enjoys about shopping for clothes. Use the letters only once. There are three extra letters which you do not need to use.

A searching for bargains

B looking at goods in windows

Speaker 1 ......

C keeping up with trends

Speaker 2 ......

D buying occasional designer items

Speaker 3 ......

E trying unusual items on

Speaker 4 ......

F finding copies of expensive items

Speaker 5 ......

G buying things for other people

H getting employee discounts

3 **Choose the correct alterative to complete the sentences about the past.**

1. I wish *I'd worn / I wore* more fashionable clothes when I was younger.
2. My brother *used to be / would be* into designer clothes but he isn't bothered about them now.
3. *Had / Have* you just come back from shopping? Where did you go?
4. I *stood / was standing* in the queue when a woman came up and pushed in front of me!
5. When I got to the shops, Mum *was already waiting / had already been waiting* for me.
6. I've *been browsing / browsed* the internet for bargains all morning.
7. I've missed the deadline for getting those cool boots in the online sale – it *has been / was* at 12 o'clock.
8. *You were / You've been* online all morning looking at clothes! Why don't we go out now?

☑ **Exam facts**

- In this part, you listen to recordings of five different people talking about a related topic.
- You have to choose which option (A–H) matches what each speaker says.

Places and buildings

1

Read the definitions and write the word.

1. a group of houses, flats or factories built in a planned way _ _ t _ _ _

2. an area inside the main entrance of a building _ o _ _ _

3. a room or set of rooms that is below ground level in a building _ _ s _ _ _ n _

4. a room under the ground floor of a building, used for storage c _ _ _ _ _

5. a long passage in a building or train _ _ r _ _ _ _ _

6. a building or area of land _ _ _ _ _ _ _ y

7. a room where an artist works, or a very small flat _ _ u _ _ _

8. a flat area outside a house or restaurant where you can sit _ _ _ _ _ c _

☑ Exam task

2

🔊 **Track 8 You will hear five short extracts in which people are talking about houses they used to live in. For questions 1–5, choose from the list (A–H) the main disadvantage of each speaker's previous house. Use the letters only once. There are three extra letters which you do not need to use.**

A   the noise

B   the temperature

C   the expense   Speaker 1 ......

D   the maintenance   Speaker 2 ......

E   the views   Speaker 3 ......

F   the location   Speaker 4 ......

G   the neighbours   Speaker 5 ......

H   the design

3a Complete the sentences with the correct form of *used to* or *be / get used to*.

1. My grandparents .... live abroad and we would visit them every summer.
2. Did you .... play 'hide and seek' at home when you were a child?
3. I'm .... living in a city, so I'd never move to the countryside.
4. I .... to like our old house 'cos it was too far from where my friends lived.
5. My sister moved out of my parents' house and is .... living on her own.
6. They .... the size of the house now, though it seemed enormous when they moved in.
7. .... you use to live next door to me when we were kids?
8. I never .... sharing a bedroom, so I'm glad I've got my own again now we've moved.

3b Match structures 1–3 with uses / meanings a–c. Use the examples to help you.

1. ***used to* + infinitive** ......

When we lived on the coast, we **used to take** our dog for long walks on the beach.

My grandparents **used to have** a big house, but a few years ago they decided to move to a smaller flat.

2. ***be used to* + *-ing* / noun** ......

I grew up in New York, so I**'m used to living** in a big city.

When my family first moved to London from Spain, I didn't like it because I **wasn't used to the weather**.

3. ***get used to* + *-ing* / noun** ......

Our new house is much bigger than the last one. We're still **getting used to having** so much space!

When we moved to a new town I had to change school, but it didn't take me long to **get used to it**.

a	become familiar with something
b	be familiar with something
c	to talk about actions that happened often in the past but no longer happen, or to talk about things that were true in the past, but are no longer true

3c Complete the sentences with your own ideas. Pay attention to the form of the verb after *used to* and *get used to*.

1. When I was younger I used to ....
2. It was difficult for me to get used to ....
3. 100 years ago, people used to ....
4. I didn't use to ....

☑ Exam tips

-   Read the instructions and the eight options (A–H) carefully and underline the most important words.
-   The eight options (A–H) don't usually follow the order of what you hear in the recording.
-   There are three options that you don't need.

Travel and holidays

1a Match the definitions with the words in the box.

amused	cheerful	dissatisfied	enthusiastic
fed up	impressed	puzzled	relieved

1. happy that something unpleasant has not happened, or has ended ....

2. showing that you think something is funny ....

3. feeling admiration or respect for someone or something ....

4. annoyed or bothered by something you have experienced for too long ....

5. feeling positive and happy ....

6. confused because you do not understand something ....

7. feeling energetic interest in something and eager to be involved in it ....

8. not pleased or happy with something ....

1b In which situations might you use these adjectives to describe how you're feeling?

☑ Exam task

2 🔊 Track 9 You will hear five short extracts in which people are talking about holiday accommodation. For questions 1–5, choose from the list (A–H) each speaker's first impression of the accommodation. Use the letters only once. There are three extra letters which you do not need to use.

A the size of the building

B how peaceful the surroundings were

C how impressive the setting was   Speaker 1 ......

D how suitable the location was   Speaker 2 ......

E how beautiful the scenery was   Speaker 3 ......

F how comfortable the furnishings were   Speaker 4 ......

G how well-equipped the accommodation was   Speaker 5 ......

H how welcoming the people were

3a Complete the sentences with words connected with flying.

1. The flight leaves from Gate 12 in T_ _ _ _ _ _ _ 3.
2. Once everyone has safely b_ _ _ _ _ _, the doors will be closed.
3. All electronic devices must be switched off while the a _ _ _ _ _ _t is in flight.
4. Air traffic control have just cleared us for t _ _ _ o _ _.
5. This is your c_ _ _ _ _ _ speaking. We are currently cruising at a height of 10,000 metres.
6. We are now making our a_ _ _ _ _ ch into Doha.
7. The plane had to make its l_ _ _ _ _ _ in stormy weather.
8. All sc_ _ _ _ _ _ d flights have been cancelled until further notice.

3b Match the words from exercise 3a with the definitions.

1. travelling at a regular time each day or week ....
2. the person who controls a ship or plane ....
3. the part of a flight when the plane starts to slowly descend towards an airport ....
4. get onto a plane or other form of public transport ....
5. the moment when a plane leaves the ground and starts to fly ....
6. any vehicle that can fly, for example, a plane or helicopter ....
7. when a plane arrives on the ground at the end of the flight ....
8. the area of an airport where you can get onto an plane ....

Get it right!

Look at the sentences below and choose the correct one.

Our holiday was very amused, and Crete was beautiful.

Our holiday was very amusing, and Crete was beautiful.

Cultures and customs

1 Complete the sentences with the words in the box.

beliefs	culture shock	diverse	dress	interpret	manners	tradition	values

1. It's considered good .... to take your shoes off before entering someone's home.

2. The tour guide had to .... for us because we couldn't speak the language.

3. My dad has strong family .... He always thinks of us before anyone else.

4. It's a .... to have firework displays at New Year.

5. I like the national .... of Ghana – it's very colourful.

6. You should respect other people's .... , even if their ideas are very different to your own.

7. When you spend time in a country that is very different to your own, you might experience ....

8. There are students from a .... range of countries in our class – there are people from all over the world.

2 Choose the correct alternative to complete the sentences.

1. The receptionist listened *patiently / carelessly* while I tried to speak Spanish to her.

2. The salsa band performed *furiously / brilliantly* – I'd never heard such amazing music!

3. The guide *eagerly / suspiciously* showed us around the ancient temple. He was very enthusiastic about it.

4. The host greeted us *warmly / nervously*, which made us feel at home immediately.

5. We looked around *proudly / curiously* – it was fascinating to visit somewhere so different.

6. I *accidentally / anxiously* made a mistake when I ate all the food on my plate – it's polite to leave a little in some countries.

7. Dan *confidently / nervously* asked for directions in Portuguese – he didn't know whether he would understand the reply.

8. We *calmly / enthusiastically* read about the traditions of Japan and couldn't wait to take part in them.

☑ **Exam task**

🔊 **Track 10** You will hear an interview with a travel writer called Anna Bryant, who is talking about what to do when visiting other countries. For questions 1–7, choose the best answer (A, B or C).

1. Before travelling to another country, Anna always tries to
   A watch people practising their traditions.
   B talk to someone from that country.
   C do some background reading.

2. How does Anna feel about her language skills?
   A regretful that she didn't pay more attention at school
   B confident that she can communicate fairly easily
   C amazed by how many languages she has acquired

3. Anna says that when visiting someone in their home
   A it's fine to let them know you're anxious.
   B it's a good idea to copy how they behave.
   C it's advisable to find out what to do in advance.

4. How did Anna feel when she made a mistake?
   A annoyed that she had forgotten some advice
   B grateful that her host was sympathic
   C amused by her own behaviour

5. How did Anna overcome culture shock when she lived abroad?
   A by studying the culture carefully
   B by getting to know local people
   C by establishing a routine

6. How did Anna feel when she was at the Lantern Festival?
   A astonished that she had never heard about it
   B anxious to remember every moment of it
   C eager to participate in it

7. What does Anna say about the book she is writing about culture?
   A She is disappointed in her progress so far.
   B She is keen to get feedback from people she knows.
   C She is unsure about including her own experiences.

☑ **Exam facts**

- In this part, you listen to a recording of two people speaking.
- You have to choose the correct answer (A, B or C) for seven questions.

© Cambridge University Press and UCLES 2015

The environment

1 How much do you know about the environment? Complete the quiz with the words at the bottom of the page to find out. Then discuss the question with a partner.

ENVIRONMENT QUIZ

1 This means not harmful to the environment. ....

2 This is the amount of energy that a person/organisation uses.
....

3 This is the word you use to describe the mixture of gases around the Earth.
....

4 This is when you make a place tidy by removing things from it.
....

5 This is a basic substance that is used in or produced by chemistry.
....

6 This word means to be likely to cause harm or damage to something or someone. ....

7 This is the increase in world temperatures caused by polluting gas.
....

8 This word means not using chemical products when growing plants for food. ....

How 'green' are you? What could you do to be more environmentally friendly?

carbon footprint	environmentally friendly	threaten
atmosphere		chemical
global warming	organic	clean up

2 ◀)) Track 11 **You will hear an interview with a boy called Liam Banks, who helped to organise a local environmental project called a clean-up day. For questions 1–7, choose the best answer (A, B or C).**

1. When did Liam decide to get involved in cleaning up his town?
   A when neighbours asked him to join in
   B when he studied the environment at school
   C when the local council asked for volunteers

2. How did Liam feel while he was looking for volunteers?
   A surprised by the amount of support he got
   B concerned about how to inform people
   C pleased to be offered free materials

3. On the morning of the clean-up, Liam felt
   A admiration for the people of his town.
   B respect for the other organisers.
   C delighted at the number of reporters there.

4. How did Liam feel when he was cleaning the pond?
   A upset at the thought of animals being harmed
   B angry at the people who had left rubbish there
   C worried about how to make sure it stayed clean

5. What disappointed Liam and the other organisers on the day?
   A volunteers complaining about the work
   B not having time to meet all the volunteers
   C forgetting to arrange food for volunteers

6. How does Liam feel about his involvement in the clean-up?
   A proud that he has made a positive difference
   B keen to organise further environmental projects
   C confident he can improve things on a wider scale

7. What advice does Liam give about becoming environmentally friendly?
   A Make small changes in behaviour.
   B Read about issues affecting the Earth.
   C Look out for local environmental events.

3 **Complete the phrasal verbs in these sentences. Use *in*, *on*, *out*, *up* or *with*.**

1. I agree .... the fact that everyone's got a part to play in reducing the impact of global warming.

2. If you present your chemical clean-up ideas to the council, I'll come along and back you ....

3. If you really believe .... making changes, you've got to do something about it.

4. Our class have come up .... some interesting ways to save water.

5. Can I count .... you to help me clean up the riverbank?

6. We've got to deal .... the issue of littering in the school grounds.

7. We need to face .... to the fact that if we don't act now, the planet will be damaged forever.

☑ **Exam tips**

- Before the recording starts, there is a pause of one minute. Use this time to read the questions and options carefully.

- Every question has a 'cue' – words that have a similar meaning to the question. This tells you that you are about to hear the answer in that part of the recording.

- The correct answer usually expresses what the speaker says using different words and phrases.

Sport

1 Complete the sentences with the words in the box. Which sport do all the words relate to? Which of the words are used for other team sports that you know about?

defender	division	opponent	penalty
pitch	referee	save	tackle

1. A .... is a person who is in charge of the game and makes sure the rules are followed.
2. A .... is an advantage given to a sports team or player when the other team or player breaks a rule.
3. A .... is someone in a sports team who tries to prevent the other team from scoring points or goals.
4. A .... contains groups of sports teams in a league.
5. Someone who you compete against in a game or competition is your ....
6. If you .... someone, you try to get the ball from someone in a game.
7. The .... is an area painted with lines for playing particular sports.
8. If you .... a goal, you prevent a player from scoring.

☑ Exam task

2 ◀)) Track 12 You will hear an interview with a springboard diver called Max Hart, who is talking about his sport. For questions 1–7, choose the best answer (A, B or C).

1. Max says that he became a diver because
   A he had competed in a similar sport.
   B it felt like the natural thing to do.
   C someone suggested he try it.

2. How did Max feel before his first competition?
   A confident that he would enjoy taking part
   B surprised by how many spectators there were
   C nervous about competing against experienced divers

3. What does Max say about doing arm stand dives?
   A He found them challenging at first.
   B He now prefers them to other dives.
   C He only performs them when he has to.

4. What was Max worried about when he had to change a dive?
   A not remembering what he had to do
   B not having had enough time to practise it
   C not being physically able to do it

5. Max enjoys his practice sessions because he
   A gets to see what everyone else is doing.
   B notices improvements in his dives every time.
   C has fun with the other students in the class.

6. What would Max like to do next?
   A take part in a major competition
   B learn to dive with a partner
   C beat his best score

7. Max enjoys diving so much because he feels
   A thrilled by the atmosphere at diving events.
   B excited when he comes first in competitions.
   C confident that he will continue to improve.

Choose the correct alternative to complete the sentences.

1. We won't win the race because there's *too much / enough* competition.
2. That shot wasn't *too good / good enough* to win the competition.
3. Martial arts are *too / enough* challenging for me.
4. Have we got *too / enough* time to train for the marathon?
5. Are we training *too hard / hard enough* to qualify?
6. The score was *too good / good enough* for me, though we could have done better.
7. I'm *too / enough* tired to go for a run this afternoon.
8. Slow down! You're running *too fast / fast enough* for me!

🎯 *Get it right!*

Look at the sentences below. Then try to correct the mistake in each one.

I don't think it's enough big.

I think it's possible to go by bike, but we don't have time enough.

Family and friends

1a **Complete the questions with the words in the box. Then match 1–4 with a–d.**

> like (x2)   alike   look like

1. What does your friend .... ?
2. What's your friend .... ?
3. What does your friend .... doing?
4. How are you and your friend .... ?

a He / She likes extreme sports and gaming.
b He / She's tall and slim, with fair hair.
c We both have a good sense of humour.
d He / She's confident and energetic.

1b **Write four sentences about a member of your family.**

Name of family member: ....
1. What's your .... like?
....
2. What does he / she look like?
....
3. What does he / she like doing?
....
4. Are you and him / her alike?
....
If so, how are you alike?
....

2a **Match 1–7 with a–g to make phrases for asking for clarification / repetition.**

1. Could you repeat
2. Sorry, I'm not sure what
3. I'm sorry, I didn't
4. Could you say that
5. Would you mind
6. Could you speak up
7. Sorry, what

a you're asking me.
b was that?
c again, please?
d the question, please?
e catch that.
f repeating what you just said?
g a little, please?

2b **Circle the word or words you *shouldn't* use in polite situations to ask for clarification or repetition.**

Pardon?   What?   Sorry?

☑ **Exam task**

3a 🔊 **Track 13** **Put the words in order to make the examiner's questions. Then listen and check.**

1. family / do / large / have / you / or / small / a / ?

   ....

2. important / life / most / people / who / in / are / the / your / ?

   ....

3. spend / you / with / family / time / your / do / how / ?

   ....

4. about / your / tell / us / good / one / friends / of / .

   ....

5. share / family / you / interests / do / your / similar / and / ?

   ....

6. you / friends / and / what / enjoy / doing / together / do / your / ?

   ....

7. friends / about / your / have / you / do / and / ideas / similar / life / ?

   ....

8. get / family / on / in / your / best / do / who / you / with / ?

   ....

3b **In pairs, ask and answer the questions in exercise 3a.**

☑ **Exam facts**

- In this part, the examiner asks you questions about yourself.
- The questions are usually about your name, hobbies, family and friends, future plans, etc.

Go to https://www.youtube.com/user/cambridgeenglishtv to watch official Cambridge English videos of *First* and *First for Schools* Speaking tests.

Hobbies and leisure

1 **Put the phrases in the correct column.**

Another thing is (that) …	Apart from that …	as / because / since
As well as that …	Obviously, it's …	The main thing is (that) …
The reason for this is (that) …		There's also the fact that …

Giving reasons	Adding reasons
……………………………………	……………………………………
……………………………………	……………………………………
……………………………………	……………………………………
……………………………………	……………………………………

2 **Choose the correct linking word to complete the sentences.**

1. *Due to the fact / Owing to* that so many people want to try surfing, we've put on some extra classes.

2. *Since / Owing to* you love gaming so much, why don't we go the new gaming hall in town?

3. The play should have been held outside, but it was cancelled *because / because of* the high winds.

4. Unfortunately, the dance class has been cancelled *because / owing to* lack of interest.

5. I think I'm going off action films, *since / so* I might not watch any more.

6. The town's really busy today *as / due to* the music festival that's taking place.

7. The match was cancelled and we *so / therefore* got our money back.

8. So many people wanted to see the film that the cinema put on another screening of it *because of / as a result*.

3a 🔊 Track 14 **Match 1–8 with a–h to make examiner's questions. Then listen and check and write the additional questions.**

1. How do you like to	**a** the news?
2. Do you prefer spending your	**b** interesting hobby?
3. What's your most	**c** done in your free time recently.
4. What kinds of books or films	**d** free time indoors or outdoors?
5. Do you enjoy going to the	**e** cinema, theatre or concerts?
6. Do you enjoy keeping up with	**f** spend your evenings and weekends?
7. How much do you enjoy parties	**g** or large social events?
8. Tell us about something interesting you've	**h** do you like.

3b **In pairs, ask and answer the questions in exercise 3a. Use linking words and give reasons for your answers.**

☑ **Exam tips**

- Answer in full sentences. Don't give one-word answers.
- If you don't understand something, ask the examiner to repeat it.
- Try to give reasons and examples in your answers.

Go to https://www.youtube.com/user/cambridgeenglishtv to watch official Cambridge English videos of *First* and *First for Schools* Speaking tests.

Education and work

1a Match 1–4 with a–d to make expressions which give you time to think.

1. That's an interesting		**a** tough one!	
2. Let me think about		**b** let me see …	
3. That's a		**c** that for a minute.	
4. I'm not sure about that –		**d** question.	

1b In pairs, talk about the following for two minutes each. Use the expressions in 1a.

1. Your favourite subject at school and what you like / liked about it
2. Your ideal job and why you'd like to do it
3. What you enjoy about learning English and why
4. How education has been useful in your life, giving an example

☑ Exam task

2a 🔊 Track 15 Complete the examiner's sentences and questions with the words in the box. Then listen and check.

ambitions	environment	kind	online	on your own	physically	project	subjects

1. What are your work or study .... ?
2. Tell us about the .... which you find most interesting.
3. Do you prefer working or studying .... or with other people?
4. What .... of work would you like to do in the future?
5. Do you prefer mentally or .... challenging work?
6. What kind of .... do you enjoy working or studying in?
7. How often do you go .... to find out about something?
8. Tell us about an interesting work or study .... you've done recently.

2b In pairs, ask and answer the questions in exercise 2a.

3 Look at the phrases. Underline the verbs which are used to talk about plans and hopes for the future. Then complete the sentences so that they are true for you. Tell your partner about your plans and hopes.

At some point in the future, I'd like to ....
....

I'm planning to ....
....

I hope that I'll ....
....

In five years' time, I expect to ....
....

Before the end of the year, I want to ....
....

This weekend, I intend to ....
....

I'm going to ....
....

I wish I could ....
....

Get it right!

Look at the sentence below. Then try to correct the mistake.

I wish I become a teacher one day. After I graduate, of course!

Go to https://www.youtube.com/user/cambridgeenglishtv to watch official Cambridge English videos of *First* and *First for Schools* Speaking tests.

Shopping

1 Complete the description of the photos using the words and phrases in the box.

both	In contrast	In the same way	main similarity
most obvious difference	nearly as nice as	whereas	while

 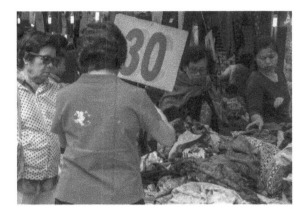

The **(1)** .... between the two pictures is that they **(2)** .... show people shopping. The **(3)** .... is where the people are shopping. The first picture shows two men window shopping. It appears to be an expensive shoe shop, **(4)** .... the people in the second picture look as if they are at a market of some kind. The market doesn't look **(5)** .... the shoe shop. It could be a second-hand clothing stall. The men in the first picture look like they're relaxed. **(6)** .... , the women in the second picture look serious. The men in the first picture might be on a day out, **(7)** .... the women in the second picture could be shopping out of necessity. It's difficult to say whether the men in the first picture will actually buy the shoes they're looking at. **(8)** .... , we don't know whether the women at the market will buy anything either.

2 Look at the modal forms in the box. Which express certainty? Which express possibility? Complete the sentences with an appropriate form from the box.

can't have	could	couldn't have	may	might	might have	must (x2)

1. It .... be a second-hand clothing stall. (possibility)
2. They .... be about to try on the hats. (possibility)
3. The boy .... need a new mobile phone. (certainty)
4. They .... bought anything – they don't have any bags. (certainty)
5. The women .... be on a shopping trip. (possibility)
6. The girls .... afforded to buy the car. They didn't have any money. (certainty)
7. The man .... left his wallet at home. (possibility)
8. It .... be a large shop because there are some lifts in the background. (certainty)

☑ **Exam task**

🔊 Track 16 **Here are some photographs of people shopping. Talk about them with a partner. Answer the questions.**

Student A, here are some photographs (1 and 2) of people shopping in different ways. What do you think are the advantages for the people of shopping in these different ways?

Photograph 1

Photograph 2

Student B, do you like shopping online? Why? / Why not?

Student B, here are some photographs (3 and 4) of people shopping for food in different places. What might the people enjoy about shopping for food in these places?

Photograph 3

Photograph 4

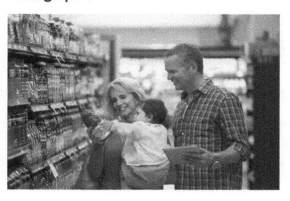

Student A, which of these places would you prefer to shop in? Why?

☑ **Exam facts**

- In this part, you are given two photos to talk about.
- You have to compare the photos and answer a question about them.
- You also have to answer a question about the other candidate's photos.

Go to https://www.youtube.com/user/cambridgeenglishtv to watch official Cambridge English videos of *First* and *First for Schools* Speaking tests.

Hobbies and leisure

1a Put the discourse markers in the correct column.

| also ... | alternatively ... | as well ... | as with ... | instead of ... |
| like ... | likewise ... | unlike ... | what's more ... |

Comparing	Contrasting	Adding
....	....	....
....	....	....
....	....	....

1b Compare the photos using the discourse markers.

2 Match 1–8 with a–h to make phrases for dealing with difficulties when speaking.

1. Sorry, I've forgotten what		**a** the word for ...	
2. What I meant		**b** I meant.	
3. I can't remember		**c** explaining myself very well.	
4. Sorry, I'm not		**d** I was about to say.	
5. What I was		**e** saying?	
6. What was I		**f** the thing that ...	
7. That's not really what		**g** trying to say was ...	
8. What do you call		**h** to say was ...	

☑ Exam task

3 🔊 **Track 17 Here are some photographs of people doing different activities. Talk about them with a partner. Answer the questions.**

Student A, here are some photographs (1 and 2) of people doing different water sports. What might attract the people to these activities?

Photograph 1

Photograph 2

Student B, which of these activities would you most like to do? Why?

Student B, here are some photographs (3 and 4) of people doing different activities. What might the people find difficult about doing these activities?

Photograph 3

Photograph 4

Student A, what creative activity would you like to be able to do? Why?

☑ Exam tips

- Don't just describe the two photos. You must say what is similar and different about them.
- If you can't remember a word, think of other words to express what you want to say. It's important that you continue talking and complete the task.
- Don't interrupt the other candidate. The examiner will ask you a question when it's your turn to speak.

Go to https://www.youtube.com/user/cambridgeenglishtv to watch official Cambridge English videos of *First* and *First for Schools* Speaking tests.

Travel and holidays

1 Complete the sentences using the phrases in the box.

doesn't look as	far more	isn't quite as
much later than	nowhere near as	the more annoyed

1. The man in the second photo looks .... bored **than** the woman in the first picture.
2. The train journey in the first picture looks .... stressful **as** the road journey in the second picture.
3. The man in the second picture .... happy **as** the woman in the first picture.
4. **The more** the man sits in traffic, ... he'll probably get.
5. Travelling by car .... comfortable **as** travelling by train.
6. The man in the car will probably arrive .... he wanted to.

2a Choose the correct alternative to complete the sentences.

1. It *looks / looks as if* the man is about to run into the sea.
2. The hotel *seems / looks* to be in a very peaceful location.
3. The tourists *look like / appear to be* lost.
4. The pool *looks / appears* really inviting. I'd love to dive in!

2b Write four sentences about the picture using *looks* (*as if / though*), *looks like*, *appears* and *seems*.

1. ....
2. ....
3. ....
4. ....

Exam task

🔊 Track 18 Here are some photographs of people on holiday. Talk about them with a partner. Answer the questions.

Student A, here are some photographs (1 and 2) of families having different kinds of holidays. Why might these families have chosen these different holidays?

Photograph 1

Photograph 2

Student B, which of these holidays would you prefer? Why?

Student B, here are some photographs (3 and 4) of people sightseeing in different ways. What do you think the people enjoy about sightseeing in these ways?

Photograph 3

Photograph 4

Student A, do you enjoy guided tours? Why? / Why not?

 Get it right!

Look at the sentence below. Then try to correct the mistake.

She looks as a shy young girl.

Go to https://www.youtube.com/user/cambridgeenglishtv to watch official Cambridge English videos of *First* and *First for Schools* Speaking tests.

Health and fitness

1 Make suggestions for getting healthier and fitter, using the phrases in the box. Use each phrase once only.

| How about ... | I suggest ... | I think we should ... | Let's ... |
| Shall we ... | We could ... | What about ... | Why don't we ... |

1. ....
2. ....
3. ....
4. ....
5. ....
6. ....
7. ....
8. ....

2 Match 1–8 with a–h. Then discuss the questions in pairs. Encourage your partner to give their opinions.

1. Do you think you need to join a gym or exercise class
2. Some people say that it can be difficult to find time
3. Do you agree that you have to spend
4. Apart from exercising and eating well,
5. How important do you think it is to choose
6. What could you say to encourage someone
7. Do you think eating meals at regular times
8. How important do you think it is to spend some

a what else can you do to stay healthy?
b who doesn't enjoy exercise or healthy food?
c time outdoors every day?
d to exercise or cook. What do you think?
e a lot of money in order to be fit and healthy?
f helps you stay healthy?
g a form of exercise that you enjoy?
h in order to get fit?

3 🔊 Track 19 **Here are some things that schools and workplaces do to encourage their students and employees to be healthier.**

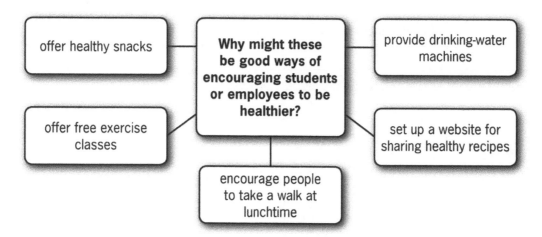

- offer healthy snacks
- offer free exercise classes
- **Why might these be good ways of encouraging students or employees to be healthier?**
- provide drinking-water machines
- set up a website for sharing healthy recipes
- encourage people to take a walk at lunchtime

Talk to each other about why these might be good ways of encouraging students or employees to be healthier. Then decide which way of encouraging students or employees to be healthier would make the most difference to them.

4 🔊 Track 20 **Listen to the examiner's questions and take turns answering them.**

☑ Exam facts

- In Part 3, you and the other candidate are given a question and five ideas.
- Together, you have to talk about the different ideas, make suggestions, agree or disagree and try to decide on an answer to the question.
- In Part 4, the examiner asks you some questions related to the topic you discussed in Part 3.

© Cambridge University Press and UCLES 2015

Go to https://www.youtube.com/user/cambridgeenglishtv to watch official Cambridge English videos of *First* and *First for Schools* Speaking tests.

Family and friends

1a Put the phrases in the correct columns.

> As far as I'm concerned, …   In my experience, …   Let me explain …
> Personally, I'd say that …   Speaking for myself, …   The reason I say this is because …
> To put it another way, …   What I mean by that is …

Giving an opinion	Clarifying an opinion
…………………………………	…………………………………
…………………………………	…………………………………
…………………………………	…………………………………
…………………………………	…………………………………

1b Then give your opinions on 1–4. Support your arguments with examples.

1. You don't need more than a couple of good friends.
2. It's important to maintain the same friendships throughout life.
3. You only find out who your real friends are when you have a problem.
4. You should talk to your family first when you need advice.

2 Match 1–8 with a–h to make concluding statements and questions.

1.	OK then, we have	**a**	on that?
2.	Shall we make our final	**b**	think that …
3.	So, we both	**c**	made a decision.
4.	What have	**d**	an agreement.
5.	I think that's it,	**e**	don't you?
6.	Are we agreed	**f**	decision now?
7.	I think we've come	**g**	we decided then?
8.	We've reached	**h**	to a conclusion about …

☑ *Exam task*

3 🔊 Track 21 **Here are some activities that families with teenage children can do together.**

- going on a long bike ride
- **What are the advantages and disadvantages for families with teenage children of doing these activities together?**
- going to watch a sports match
- going to a concert
- playing video games
- visiting historical sites

Talk to each other about the advantages and disadvantages for families with teenage children of doing these activities together. Then decide which activity you think is best for bringing families with teenage children closer together.

4 🔊 Track 22 **Listen to the examiner's questions and take turns answering them.**

☑ *Exam tips*

- In Part 3, you must talk to the other candidate and not the examiner.
- You should talk about three or four of the ideas with the other candidate. Don't try to reach a decision too quickly.
- To keep the conversation going, use phrases like *What do you think?* or *Shall we move on to the next one?*
- In Part 4, you should try to give extended answers, with details and examples supporting your ideas.

Go to https://www.youtube.com/user/cambridgeenglishtv to watch official Cambridge English videos of *First* and *First for Schools* Speaking tests.

Education and study

1 **Do these phrases express agreement or disagreement? How strong are they?**

I agree to a large extent.	I couldn't agree more.	I'd say the exact opposite.
I'm not sure about that.	I partly agree.	I totally disagree.
	No doubt about it.	No way.

100% agree ....

....

....

....

....

....

....

100% disagree ....

2 **Give your opinions about the following. Use the phrases from exercise 1 and give reasons for your answers.**

1. It's impossible to get a good job if you don't go to university.
2. There's no point studying subjects you don't like at school.
3. Subjects like philosophy and psychology should be studied from a young age.
4. Getting good grades isn't important if you've tried your best.

3a **Complete the phrases with the words in the box.**

account	although	balance	general	hand	sides	tend	whole

1. On ...., I'd say that ....
2. On the ...., I believe that ....
3. I .... to think that ....
4. In ...., I believe that ....
5. On the one ...., on the other ....
6. .... I think ...., I also think ....
7. I can understand both .... of the argument, so ....
8. Taking everything into ...., ...

3b **When might you use these phrases? Finish the sentences so that they are true for you, using your ideas from exercise 2.**

4 🔊 **Track 23** **Here are some activities that people learning English can do to improve their speaking skills.**

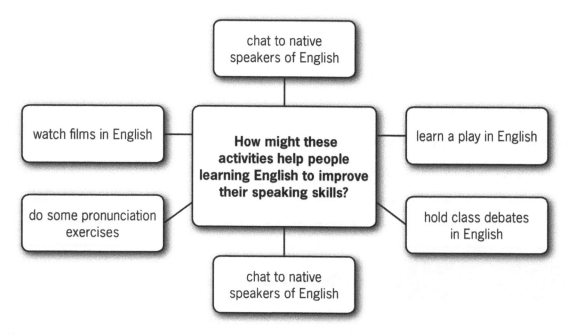

Talk to each other about how these activities might help people learning English to improve their speaking skills. Then decide which activity would be least helpful to people learning English.

5 🔊 **Track 24** **Listen to the examiner's questions and take turns answering them.**

Look at the sentence below. Then try to correct the mistake.

I think you will be agree with me.

Go to https://www.youtube.com/user/cambridgeenglishtv to watch official Cambridge English videos of *First* and *First for Schools* Speaking tests.

First Reading and Use of English Part 1

Read the sentences about First Reading and Use of English Part 1. Are they TRUE or FALSE?

1. Part 1 tests your knowledge of how to use lexis (words and phrases) rather than grammar. ....

2. To complete the gaps in the text, you have to choose from three word options. ....

3. The options you choose from may be words or phrases that are quite similar in meaning. ....

4. There is an example at the beginning of the task. ....

5. Sometimes more than one answer may be correct. ....

6. There are ten questions in the task. ....

7. Phrasal verbs may be tested in Part 1. ....

8. The reading text is about 300 words long. ....

 First Reading and Use of English Part 2

Complete the sentences about First Reading and Use of English Part 2 with the words from the box. There are four words or numbers you do not need.

eight	example	grammar	linkers	phrase	option
six	topics	vocabulary	word	240	160

The focus of the Part 2 task is **(1)** .... You have to complete a text containing missing words

such as prepositions, verb forms, **(2)** .... and articles. There are **(3)** .... gaps to fill.

The first sentence of the text contains a gap with an **(4)** .... Most sentences in the text will have

a missing **(5)** .... The text you have to read will be no more than **(6)** .... words long.

Part 2 texts can be about a variety of **(7)** .... including daily life, education, work, sport, science

and technology, but will not contain difficult or technical **(8)** ....

First Reading and Use of English Part 3

Complete the sentences about First Reading and Use of English Part 3 with the correct alternatives.

1. In Part 3 the text you read is about *160 / 220* words long.

2. The focus of the task is *tense formation / word formation*.

3. You have to answer *eight / twelve* questions.

4. You answer each question by *filling in a gap / choosing an A, B, or C option*.

5. You must change a *sentence / word* into another form to answer each question.

6. You need to pay special attention to *spelling / punctuation* in this task.

7. You are often tested on your knowledge of *prepositions / prefixes* in this part of the exam.

8. You can make a maximum of *one change / two changes* to the word you are given.

 First Reading and Use of English Part 4

Read the sentences about First Reading and Use of English Part 4. Are they TRUE or FALSE?

1. In Part 4 you will read sentences rather than a text. ....

2. The sentences in the task will all be about the same topic. ....

3. Part 4 tests the ability to use lexical and grammatical structures. ....

4. You have to complete eight sentences in the task. ....

5. You have to change each sentence into another that has the same meaning. ....

6. In each question you are given a key word which you must use in your answer. ....

7. As in Part 3, the key word given can be changed to a different form. ....

8. You must complete the gap in the second sentence with between three and six words. ....

Think about it   First Reading and Use of English Part 5

Match 1–8 with a–h to make sentences about First Reading and Use of English Part 5.

1. Part 5 consists of a text followed by

2. Part 5 is a multiple-

3. Each question has

4. The text can be an article or an extract from

5. The questions may focus on detailed

6. The questions may also test your comprehension of the writer's

7. Questions may test your comprehension of reference words in the text such as

8. You may also have to work out the meaning of a word or phrase

a   opinion or attitude, which may be inferred rather than stated.

b   pronouns.

c   from its context.

d   four options.

e   a modern novel.

f   choice task.

g   six questions.

h   understanding or the main ideas of the text.

Think about it   First Reading and Use of English Part 6

Complete the text about First Reading and Use of English Part 6 with the correct word or phrase from the box.

individual sentences	signalling and linking	more than one	have been removed
articles	answer options	numbered gap	does not fit

The texts for Part 6 are usually **(1)** .... from magazines or newspapers, or informative

texts. Following the text, there is a box with seven sentences in it. These are the **(2)** ....

Six of the seven sentences **(3)** .... from the text, and all seven are in a random order.

The exam questions are gaps numbered one to six in the text. You have to decide which sentence belongs in which

(4) .... The seventh sentence in the box **(5)** .... in any of

the gaps. You may not use any sentence for **(6)** .... question.

To do this task well, you have to focus on how texts are structured, rather than concentrating on

(7) .... This means you will need to follow the development of ideas, opinions and

events through the text as a whole. For this reason, a good understanding of **(8)** ....

devices in a text is essential for this part of the exam.

Think about it First Reading and Use of English Part 7

Read the text about First Reading and Use of English Part 7. Are they TRUE or FALSE?

Part 7 is the final part of the Reading and Use of English paper and consists of one long text with several paragraphs, or up to six shorter texts. It is preceded by ten questions. Candidates are required to locate the specific information which matches the questions. To do this, they need to understand detail, attitude or opinion in the question and locate a section of text where that idea is expressed, discounting ideas in other sections which may appear similar but which do not reflect the whole of the question accurately. Some of the options may be correct for more than one question.

1. There may be six short texts in this part of the test. ....

2. There may be one text in this part containing up to six paragraphs. ....

3. You need to understand what the writer of the text thinks to do this task well. ....

4. There is only one question for each text in this part of the test. ....

5. There are between six and ten questions in this part of the reading exam. ....

6. Some parts of the text may contain words, information or ideas that look like the answer to the question but say something a little different. ....

7. The questions are positioned before the text on the paper. ....

8. This is the last part of the Reading and Use of English paper. ....

 Think about it First Writing Part 1

Complete the sentences about First Writing Part 1 with the correct alternatives.

1. In Part 1, you have to write *a story / an essay* about a particular topic.

2. The task gives *two / three* points you must discuss in your essay.

3. You *must / don't have to* add your own ideas as well.

4. You should write between 140 and *160 / 190* words.

5. It *is / isn't* important to write the correct number of words, or you may get a lower mark.

6. You *should / mustn't* discuss different opinions and points of view on the topic.

7. Your essay should be organised into clear *paragraphs / numbered sections*.

8. Your essay should end with *a conclusion / a conclusion and your opinion*.

First Writing Part 2

Read the sentences about First Writing Part 2. Are they TRUE or FALSE?

1. In Part 2, you can choose what kind of writing task you do. ....

2. You can choose tasks such as writing a letter, an article, a review or an essay. ....

3. It is important to read the task carefully and include all the points or ideas that are mentioned.
....

4. Different tasks may specify that you should write different numbers of words. ....

5. It is important to think about who you are writing for, and what style you should use in your answer.
....

6. You should use formal or informal language in your answer, depending on the type of task. ....

7. It is important to organise your writing in clear paragraphs or sections, and use linking words to link your ideas.
....

8. You should try to use a good range of vocabulary, expressions and grammar in your writing.
....

 First Listening Part 1

Read the sentences about First Listening Part 1. Are they TRUE or FALSE?

1. You may hear one or two speakers. ....

2. You will hear seven different texts. ....

3. For each question, there are three options for you to choose from (A, B or C). ....

4. Some of the questions focus on the opinions or feelings of the speaker(s). ....

5. The options for each question are always presented in the same order as you hear related information. ....

6. You will hear exactly the same words as you read in the options. ....

7. You will receive one mark for each correct answer. ....

8. Sometimes you may have to decide whether two speakers agree with each other. ....

Think about it First Listening Part 2

Complete the text about First Listening Part 2 with the words from the box. Use each word once only.

answer	changes	marks	minutes	order	phrase	presentation	sentences

In Part 2, you will hear one person talking. This talk may be a **(1)** .... or another kind of monologue

and it lasts for about three **(2)** .... As you listen, you have to complete ten **(3)** ....

about the talk. Each sentence has one gap, and you have to write a word or short **(4)** .... in each

gap, according to what you hear. The information in the sentences is presented in the same **(5)** ....

as the information you hear. You should write exactly the words you hear which fit the meaning of the sentence,

without making any **(6)** .... to the words. You should try to spell the words correctly, as you may lose

(7) .... for incorrect spelling. You will receive one mark for each correct **(8)** ....

 Think about it First Listening Part 3

Match 1–8 with a–h to make sentences about First Listening Part 3.

1. In Part 3, you will hear

2. Each speaker is talking about

3. Each monologue lasts for about

4. You will see eight possible options

5. You should choose one option

6. You have to answer the same

7. There are three options which you

8. You will receive one mark

a   to choose from.

b   for each correct answer.

c   the same topic.

d   per speaker.

e   do not need to use.

f   30 seconds.

g   question for each speaker.

h   five speakers.

Think about it First Listening Part 4

Complete the sentences about First Listening Part 4 with the correct alternatives.

1. In Part 4 you hear *one / two* speakers.

2. You have to answer *six / seven* questions.

3. Each question has *three / four* options to choose from.

4. The questions *follow / may not follow* the order of the information you hear.

5. The options *will be / may not be* presented in the same order as the related information you hear.

6. There is *a short pause / no pause* between each question.

7. You *may / won't* have to understand a speaker's opinions and attitudes.

8. You will receive *one / two* mark(s) for each correct answer.

Think about it First Speaking Part 1

Complete the text about First Speaking Part 1 with the words from the box. Use each word once only.

conversation	information	interview	life	live	minutes	partner	reasons

In Part 1, you will have a **(1)** .... with the examiner. This is known as the **(2)** .... task. The examiner will ask you some questions about you and your **(3)** .... These may include questions about your hobbies and interests, work or study, where you **(4)** .... , your family, and so on. You should answer the questions providing as much **(5)** .... as you can, giving examples and **(6)** .... for your answers where appropriate. You do not need to talk to your **(7)** .... during this part of the test. Part 1 of the First Speaking test will last for about two **(8)** ....

Think about it First Speaking Part 2

Read the following sentences about First Speaking Part 2. Are they TRUE or FALSE?

1. The examiner will give you two photographs to compare. ....

2. The photographs will be connected in some way. ....

3. You will have a conversation with the examiner about the photographs. ....

4. The examiner will ask you to talk about the photographs in a particular way. For example, you might talk about the advantages for the people in the photos of an activity they are doing. ....

5. The question you have to answer is shown above the photos as a reminder. ....

6. You have to speak for about one minute without interruption. ....

7. Your partner will not comment on your photos. ....

8. The process is repeated, with your partner looking at some different photos. ....

Think about it First Speaking Part 3/4

Match 1–8 with a–h to make sentences about First Speaking Parts 3 and 4.

1. In Part 3, you will have a conversation with   a   for you to discuss.

2. The examiner will give you some material to   b   questions for you to discuss.

3. You will see some written prompts and a question   c   with the other candidate.

4. You should talk about the ideas with the other candidate   d   make a decision.

5. After this, the examiner will ask you to   e   you did in Part 3.

6. In Part 4, the examiner will ask   f   look at, and a task to do.

7. The questions are related to the task   g   for two minutes.

8. You can agree or disagree   h   the other candidate.

ANSWER KEY

Reading and Use of English Part 1:1

1a 1 on 2 in 3 by 4 into
5 about 6 with 7 to 8 at

1b 1 keen on 4 addicted to
2 brilliant at 5 got into
3 excited about

2 1 spectators 2 part 3 took
4 exhibition 5 giving 6 moving
7 plots 8 sociable

3 1 C 2 A 3 D 4 B
5 C 6 A 7 C 8 B

Reading and Use of English Part 1:2

1 1 among 2 around 3 beneath
4 back 5 along 6 beyond
7 through 8 within

2 1 travel 2 outlook 3 embarked
4 luggage 5 fee 6 cabin
7 voyage 8 programmed

3 Student's own answers.

4 1 B 2 C 3 A 4 D
5 C 6 B 7 D 8 A

Reading and Use of English Part 1:3

1 1 go 2 take 3 keeping 4 plays
5 hit 6 do 7 beat 8 develop

2a 1 playing 2 doing 3 to take up
4 going 5 to win 6 to join
7 entering 8 to lose

2b Students' own answers.

3 1 B 2 A 3 D 4 B
5 C 6 B 7 A 8 D

Get it right!
When I was at primary school, I enjoyed **playing**
basketball.

Reading and Use of English Part 2:1

1 1 an 2 every 3 all 4 Those
5 few 6 much 7 the 8 that

2 1 least 2 get / become 3 of
4 is 5 to 6 out
7 neither 8 Whatever

3a 1 c 2 b 3 c 4 a
5 c 6 b 7 a 8 b

3b 1 There aren't many days **when** I don't (Student's
own answers)
2 By the time I was ten, there weren't many (Student's
own answers) **which / that** I hadn't tried.

3 A sports person **who / that** I admire is (Student's
own answers)

4 (Student's own answers) is a country **which /
that / where** I would like to visit.

Reading and Use of English Part 2:2

1 1 As long as 5 Despite
2 Although 6 owing to
3 as well as 7 therefore
4 in order to 8 Whereas

2 1 which 2 with
3 Although / Though / While / Whilst
4 what 5 any 6 take 7 such 8 be

3a 1 make 2 apply 3 study 4 pass
5 obtain 6 go into 7 set 8 make

3b 1 took / sat / did 3 taken / enrolled on / done
2 hand in / do 4 attend; leave

Reading and Use of English Part 2:3

1a 1 myself 2 mine 3 My 4 me

1b 1 our 2 each 3 ours 4 themselves

2 1 without 5 for
2 though / if / when 6 no / little
3 because 7 who
4 another 8 same

3a 1 gets on with 5 broke up
2 get together 6 count on
3 bring up 7 fell out
4 take after 8 look up to

3b 1 get on with 4 fallen out
2 take after 5 look up to
3 get together

Get it right!
Some of **my** other friends phoned and wrote to me.
We didn't use to have our own toys – we used to share
them with **each other**.

Reading and Use of English Part 3:1

1 1 successful 5 logical
2 challenging 6 accessible
3 scientific 7 convinced
4 predictable 8 mysterious

2 1 strengthen 5 effective
2 proof 6 productive
3 impressive 7 accuracy
4 safety 8 succeed

3 1 sensitive 5 possibility
2 investigations 6 comfortable
3 significant 7 dependent
4 considerably 8 unrealistic

4 Students' own answers.

Reading and Use of English Part 3:2

1 1 reaction
2 similarity
3 feeling
4 knowledge
5 government
6 preference
7 tiredness
8 performance

2 1 fashionable
2 pleasure
3 admission
4 beneficial
5 energetic
6 Increasingly
7 impolite
8 consumption

3a 1 argument
2 imagination
3 intention
4 analysis
5 publication
6 comparison
7 description
8 preference

3b 1 consider
2 appear
3 time
4 confuse
5 arrange
6 behave
7 survive
8 respond

Reading and Use of English Part 3:3

1 1 inaccurate
2 disapprove
3 inadequate
4 unaffected
5 disappearance
6 impractical
7 misbehaved
8 discouraged

2 1 illegal
2 dissatisfied
3 irreversible
4 immature
5 irresponsible
6 dissimilar
7 irreplaceable
8 illegible

3 1 depth
2 unusual
3 endangered
4 establishment
5 unforgettable
6 accessible
7 inhabitants
8 Surprisingly

4

dis-	disapprove discourage dissimilar dissatisfied	ir-	irreversible irresponsible irreplaceable
il-	illegal illegible	mis-	misbehave
im-	impractical immature	un-	unaffected unusual unforgettable
in-	inaccurate inadequate inhabitable		

Get it right!
Nowadays, zoos are considered by many people to be **useless** and cruel.

Reading and Use of English Part 4:1

1 1 g
2 f
3 e
4 a
5 d
6 c
7 h
8 b

2 1 more; than
2 as much
3 fewer
4 less
5 as fluently / well
6 less carefully
7 as many
8 comparison

3 1 Nobody gave **a reason for the delay** to the flight.
2 This year's holiday by the sea **wasn't / was not as exciting as** last year's skiing holiday.
3 Maria says **there's / there is no / little point (in) visiting** the museum because it's not very interesting.
4 Everyone **is looking forward to** our trip to China next month.
5 When I was in Sweden, I was **able to pick up** some Swedish.
6 The architecture here **reminds me** of the buildings in Amsterdam.

Reading and Use of English Part 4:2

1 1 John promised his sister he would meet her at seven.
2 The manager said to Lucas that he had arrived late to work twice that week.
3 Rachel told her friend that she was going on a business trip to Japan.
4 Gerorge told Jessica that if they left now, they wouldn't be late.
5 Micah told his brother that they would have to tidy up the house.
6 At the job interview, the man said he had a lot of work experience.

2 1 If Leila goes to bed early, it **makes a (big) difference to** how she feels the next morning.
2 Max was still late for work **in spite of the fact** (that) he took the early bus.
3 Last year I decided **to give up eating / having** fast food for lunch.
4 Melanie goes jogging **as well as answering** her important emails before breakfast.
5 I must **get my television fixed / repaired / mended** as soon as possible.
6 Clara says **it's / it is unusual for her to** go out at the weekend.

3a 1 where his keys were
2 she was going to the party
3 he had been to the new department store
4 he would be late home on Tuesday

3b 1 Are you willing to work on Saturday?
2 Can you do the shopping on your way home?
3 Do you want to play football in the garden?
4 How long have you been off work?

Reading and Use of English Part 4:3

1 1 The heavy snow **led to some schools closing** for a couple of days.

2 Steve doesn't **pay (much) attention to** the weather forecast.

3 John **regrets not taking** an umbrella to work this morning.

4 Donna said that **with the exception of** Friday, every day last week had been really hot.

5 We've **never had weather as bad** as this in July.

6 The **heat / temperature / hot weather must have been** unbearable where you were staying.

2 1 put off
2 making out
3 put up with
4 keep up with
5 set off
6 turned out
7 get away
8 soaking up

3 1 go
2 had taken / 'd taken
3 will get
4 spent
5 would have been
6 is
7 would miss
8 won't be able / will not be able

Get it right!
She asked herself what would have happened if she hadn't caught that bus.

Reading and Use of English Part 5:1

1 1 C   2 B   3 C
4 C   5 A   6 D

2 1 search engine
2 instant messaging
3 hard drive
4 back up
5 high-tech
6 interactive games
7 Virtual reality
8 social media

Reading and Use of English Part 5:2

1 1 B   2 C   3 B
4 B   5 A   6 D

2 1 going to have
2 continues
3 will be
4 will be communicating
5 will have equipped
6 will be measuring
7 will even be able to

Reading and Use of English Part 5:3

1 1 D   2 A   3 A
4 C   5 A   6 D

2 1 I hope to get / hope I will get a promotion this year.
2 If only Josh hadn't been late so many times, he might not / wouldn't have lost his job.
3 Kathy wishes she were / was a doctor.
4 I hope Mark doesn't go to work abroad.
5 Everyone wishes (that) Leo Patten were the new boss (not / instead of Nick) / Everyone wishes (that) the new boss was / were Leo Patten.

6 If only most employers gave / would give employees eight week's holiday a year!

Get it right!
I wish you **had been** there; it was fantastic!

Reading and Use of English Part 6:1

1 1 E   2 G   3 A
4 C   5 D   6 F

2 1 should
2 may
3 do not have to
4 must not
5 should not
6 should
7 can
8 do not have to

Reading and Use of English Part 6:2

1 1 E   2 A   3 D
4 G   5 B   6 C

2 1 walking
2 fitness
3 give in
4 pace
5 stage
6 beat
7 catch up
8 marathon

3 1 must   2 let   3 should   4 mind
5 better   6 could   7 Would   8 Could

Reading and Use of English Part 6:3

1 1 E   2 G   3 D
4 A   5 B   6 F

2 1 educational
2 evidence
3 researchers
4 institution
5 argument
6 scientifically
7 valuable
8 cultural

3 1 must
2 would
3 needn't
4 can
5 needs
6 can
7 should
8 shan't

Get it right!
You are doing well in your studies in science and maths and you **could** become a doctor one day.

Reading and Use of English Part 7:1

1 1 are told / have been told
2 were stopped
3 was fought
4 was banned
5 were locked
6 were allowed
7 was introduced
8 has been attended

2 1 D   2 A   3 C   4 B   5 A
6 C   7 B   8 A   9 C   10 D

Reading and Use of English Part 7:2

1 1 When members of the audience enter the theatre, they have their tickets checked.
2 When stars drive to the hotel, they have their cars driven to the car park.
3 Nearly every time famous people go out, they get their photo taken.
4 When authors write a bestseller, they get it edited.
5 Famous people write autobiographies and (they) get them published.
6 Before actors go on stage they have their make-up done.

2 1 C   2 E   3 A   4 C   5 E
6 B   7 D   8 E   9 A   10 B

Reading and Use of English Part 7:3

1 1 It is (sometimes) said / claimed / thought global conservation is fighting a losing battle.
2 It is predicted / thought / claimed that 11% of animals worldwide will be endangered by 2050.
3 It is not known how many insect species have already become extinct.
4 It is predicted / thought / claimed that numbers of farmland birds will continue to rise.
5 It is thought / claimed that the word *butterfly* may originate from people calling one species a 'butter-coloured-fly'.
6 It is thought / claimed a new species of frog has been discovered in a remote area of jungle.

2 1 C   2 D   3 B   4 A   5 E
6 B   7 E   8 D   9 A   10 C

Get it right!

It is **said** that animals suffer a lot if they are kept in cages or behind fences.

Writing Part 1:1

1 1 In my   5 see
2 believe   6 say
3 seems   7 would
4 view   8 Personally

2 *Sample answer*
Nowadays, video games are very popular, and some young people spend a lot of time playing them, either alone or with their friends. Although there are some benefits to these games, there are also some disadvantages too.
It is possible to learn some important skills from video games. In many games, players have to make decisions quickly and decide on the best way to solve problems, often in very difficult situations. Moreover, some games can help young people to learn about different periods in history or different parts of the world in a fun way.

However, most people would agree that it isn't good to spend too much time sitting in front of a screen. It is important to be active and do plenty of exercise in order to be healthy. Young people also need to go out so they can meet new people and make friends in the real world.
To sum up, I would say that video games are a fun way to relax, have fun and learn useful skills, but it is important for young people to go out and have other hobbies too.

3 1 For instance   5 For this reason
2 As for   6 therefore
3 Moreover   7 Furthermore
4 In this way   8 To sum up

Writing Part 1:2

1 1 b   2 a   3 a
4 b   5 b   6 a

2 *Sample answer*
People are now living for longer, but many suffer from health problems that are caused by our modern way of life. It is therefore important to teach young people how to live healthy lives. While schools have an important role to play, I do not think they can teach young people everything they need to know.
Schools can certainly educate young people about the importance of exercise. Many schools already provide exercise classes and organise sports teams and games. In addition, schools can teach young people about a healthy diet, and could provide cookery lessons so young people learn how to prepare healthy meals.
However, I believe that parents, families and communities also have a responsibility to show young people how to live a healthy life. For example, parents can provide more healthy meals at home, and towns could build more sports centres and cycle lanes to encourage people to become more active.
To sum up, I agree that schools should teach young people about exercise and healthy eating, but I also believe that other people and organisations in society should help to encourage a healthy lifestyle.

3 1 Although   5 despite
2 whereas   6 While
3 On the other hand   7 in spite of
4 However   8 Nevertheless

Writing Part 1:3

1 1 b   2 j   3 e   4 f   5 g
6 c   7 d   8 a   9 i   10 h
2 1 a   2 c   3 b
4 a; c   5 b   6 c

Paragraph b is best concluding paragraph because it briefly summarises the arguments from the main paragraphs, then expresses the writer's opinion.

3 *Sample answer*
The world faces some very serious environmental problems now, such as pollution and global warming. I believe that governments around the world definitely need to do more to help the environment.
Firstly, in some cities, the pollution from cars is so bad that it is making people ill. I think governments should stop people using their cars in cities and should spend more money on public transport.
Secondly, governments need to take action to prevent global warming. For example, they could spend more money on clean forms of energy such as solar power and wind power. These are much better for the environment than using gas or oil.
However, making these changes costs a lot of money, and it is not possible for governments to pay to solve all these problems. Individuals must take responsibility and do what they can. For example, individuals can recycle things, and can save energy by switching off lights and computers when they are not using them. To conclude, I believe that governments and individuals need to work together to create a better future for everyone.

Get it right!
In conclusion / To conclude, I think life nowadays is better than it was in the past.

Writing Part 2:1

1
1 rush hour	5 scheduled
2 traffic jam	6 terminal
3 overtake	7 connection
4 lane	8 landing

2
1 As soon as	6 as
2 for some time	7 at the same time
3 later	8 immediately
4 At first	9 finally
5 before long	

3 *Sample answer*
A perfect place to relax
Last year I spent two weeks in the south of Spain with my family, and it was the best, most relaxing holiday ever! It was just after my exams, and I had been working very hard, so I was feeling exhausted.
As soon as we arrived at our hotel, I knew it was going to be perfect. The hotel was right by the beach, and all I could see in front of me was sand and sea. We put our bags in our rooms and went down to the beach immediately. The sea was lovely and warm, and before long I started to forget all about studying and exams. We didn't just go to the beach every day. We visited some local towns too, and went walking in the mountains one day. We also went on a boat trip and saw dolphins – can you imagine that? But the best thing of all was that there was no internet connection there, so for two weeks I couldn't contact my friends or talk about the exams! It really was the perfect place to forget about the world and just relax!

Writing Part 2:2

1
1 recommend	6 Would you like
2 if you like	7 must
3 worth	8 good idea
4 If I were you	9 How about
5 Why don't	10 could always

Fabio and Ana offer help.

2
1 Hello, How are things?, Hi, Great to hear from you!
2 Write soon, See you soon
3 uncle's, we'll, I've, weather's
4 I reckon
5 Plus
6 Do you fancy … ?
7 Should be fun!
8 pretty

3 *Sample answer*
Hi Rob,
Great to hear from you!
My favourite festival takes place in Ivrea, a town in the north of Italy. It happens every year in February as part of the carnival celebrations. It's called the Battle of the Oranges, and basically it's a big food fight in the street! There are nine teams of people, and they throw oranges at each other. No one really understands the origin of this festival, but it's very old. It can be pretty dangerous, so young kids aren't allowed to join in, but last year my dad and I took part for the first time, and it was amazing fun! I love this festival because it's so crazy, and because the whole town joins in – nearly a thousand people take part, and loads more watch, although you need to be careful when you're watching that you keep a safe distance away, so you don't get hit! I also love it because it makes everyone laugh, so everyone's really happy. And at the end of the day everyone goes to restaurants with their friends or families to have a special meal and celebrate.
Good luck with your project!
Claudio

Writing Part 2:3

1
1 academic	5 graduate
2 institution	6 qualify
3 seminar	7 sit
4 campus	8 lecturer

Sentences 6 and 8 are false. In Britain, it takes five years of study to qualify as a doctor. A lecturer is a university teacher who gives talks to large groups of students.

2 *Sample answer*

Dear Sir or Madam,

I am writing to apply for a job in one of your summer camps this summer.

I believe I would be suitable for this job because I am very friendly, outgoing and sociable, and I have a good sense of humour. I get on well with people of all ages, and especially with children. I often organise birthday parties for my nephews and nieces. I arrange a variety of games and activities for them, and also do magic tricks to entertain them, which are always very popular.

I am also very keen on sport. I play football and tennis regularly, and enjoy cycling and swimming too. As well as playing football, I also help coach young children at my football club and have a Level 1 qualification in sports coaching.

Because of my experience and qualifications, I think I would be a perfect candidate for this job, and hope you will consider my application. I look forward to hearing from you.

Yours sincerely,

Hannah Tomkins

3a 1 which
2 where
3 when
4 who
5 whose
6 where
7 which
8 who

a Defining relative clauses: sentences 1, 4, 6 and 7. Non-defining relative clauses: sentences 2, 3, 5 and 8.
b Sentences 1 and 7
c Sentences 1, 4 and 7

3b 1 which
2 who / that
3 – / that / which
4 whose
5 – / when
6 where
7 who
8 – / that / who

Writing Part 2:4

1 1 fantastic
2 dreadful
3 impressive
4 bizarre
5 delightful
6 genuine
7 entertaining
8 poor
9 brilliant

2 *Sample answer*

Fashion4U.uk

I'm a big fan of online shopping, and I visit a lot of online clothes shops. My absolute favourite is Fashion4U.uk.

On this website, you'll find a huge range of really fashionable clothes. There's everything from jeans and T-shirts to formal dresses and suits. They also have a fantastic selection of shoes. The site is incredibly easy to use, and you can search for clothes according to the size, colour or style you're looking

for. The prices are brilliant, too. I bought a pair of trousers there last month, then saw exactly the same pair in a local department store for twice the price! Once you've placed your order, they are usually very quick to deliver. You can even choose same-day delivery if you need the clothes quickly, although you have to pay extra for this. Unlike many other online stores, you can also phone and talk to someone if you have any problems. I've done this a few times, and I've always found them very helpful.

This is a fantastic website, and I'd thoroughly recommend it to anyone who loves clothes and loves a bargain!

3 1 would
2 advise
3 a visit
4 shopping around
5 recommend
6 definitely
7 thoroughly
8 you to buy

Writing Part 2:5

1a 1 putting up
2 be provided
3 to have
4 would be able
5 be pulled down
6 to turn/turning
7 opening
8 be improved

1b Students' own answers.

2 *Sample answer*

Introduction

This report looks at the leisure facilities available in this town and makes recommendations for improvements to these facilities and new facilities that could be provided. The information comes from an interview with students at Central Language School.

Current facilities

There are two sports centres in the town, and both can be reached easily by public transport. However, neither sports centre has a swimming pool.

The only cinema is outside the town, and can only be reached by car. This makes it difficult for people who rely on public transport.

There is a small park near the town centre, but this is often very crowded during good weather in summer.

Recommendations

I would recommend building a swimming pool at one of the sports centres. Both have plenty of land to make this possible. I would also suggest introducing a new bus route to the cinema to allow young people to reach the cinema easily. Finally, it would be beneficial to young people to make the park bigger, as this would give them more space to meet their friends in good weather.

3 1 The new sports centre opened in June.
2 What facilities are available?
3 That's terrible news!
4 "I'm going to the gym," she said.

5 The most popular sports are football, tennis and rugby.

6 If they opened a new cinema, a lot of people would go to it.

7 Although there is a youth club, not many people use it.

8 Finally, I would recommend building a new swimming pool.

Writing Part 2:6

1
1 stood	7 said
2 was waiting / waited	8 asked
3 had called	9 was watching
4 hadn't given	10 had been
5 didn't know	11 was holding
6 came	12 shouted

2 *Sample answer*

When Max opened the letter, he was so excited that that he started dancing around the room. "I won the competition! We're going to Hollywood!" he shouted. Six weeks earlier, Max had written a film script for a film-making competition. The prize was a trip to Hollywood with his family. Max was passionate about films, so this was like a dream come true for him.

When the day came to set off, Max was nervous that something would go wrong. They arrived at the airport early, to make sure they didn't miss their flight. In fact, everything went smoothly, and ten hours later they landed in America.

Hollywood was incredible! Max loved the film sets, and watching famous film directors in action. But the highlight of the trip was when they met the actor Ben Smith unexpectedly as he was getting ready for his next scene. He was really friendly, and offered Max lots of advice and encouragement.

When Max arrived back home two weeks later, he couldn't wait to tell his friends about everything that he had seen and done. It had been an amazing adventure!

3
1 impatiently	5 proudly
2 furiously	6 unexpectedly
3 cheerfully	7 honestly
4 confidently	8 nervously

Listening Part 1:1

1 1 Are you in education at the moment? Yes, I am / No, I'm not. (Students' own answers.)

2 Did you have a favourite teacher at school? Yes, I did / No, I didn't. (Students' own answers.)

3 Is there a subject you'd like to know more about? Yes, there is / No, there isn't. (Students' own answers.)

4 Have you ever found a subject challenging? Yes, I have / No, I haven't. (Students' own answers.)

5 Can you speak more than two languages? Yes, I can / No, I can't. (Students' own answers.)

6 Should creative subjects like art be taught in schools? Yes, they should / No, they shouldn't. (Students' own answers.)

7 Would you choose to study different subjects if you could? / If you could, would you choose to study different subjects? Yes, I would / No, I wouldn't. (Students' own answers.)

8 Do you enjoy learning about maths and science? Yes, I do / No, I don't. (Students' own answers.)

2
1 h	2 c	3 a	4 f
5 e	6 d	7 g	8 b

3
1 C	2 A	3 B	4 B
5 A	6 C	7 C	8 B

Narrator: 🔊 Track 1 Listening Part 1, Worksheet 1.

You will hear people talking in eight different situations. For questions 1–8, choose the best answer (A, B or C).

Narrator: **Question 1. You hear a woman telling her son about her favourite school teacher.**

Boy: Did you have a favourite teacher at school, Mum?

Woman: Good question! ... I remember we had this history teacher, Mr Evans, ... I was fascinated by the way he taught. He was just so into history. I could listen to him talk for hours and everything he said would stick with me, even if I didn't write anything down. Sometimes he'd read an account of an event aloud and although he was no actor, somehow I felt like I'd gone right back in time, to when the action was happening. He was pretty serious – I don't remember laughing the way I did in other classes – but I loved every minute.

Narrator: Now listen again.

Narrator: **Question 2. You hear a girl talking about maths.**

Girl: People often ask why I like maths so much, and if I find it easy. Well, no, I don't. But if it wasn't a challenge, I wouldn't be half as excited about it. I can spend hours working on a single maths problem – I don't give up till I've got the right answer. And that's the great thing about maths – it's either right or wrong. If you work hard enough, you can always get a hundred per cent and that's so satisfying. Some mathematicians talk about how 'maths

---

	is everywhere' – that it's relevant to everything you do in life – but I just love it for its own sake.
Narrator:	Now listen again.
Narrator:	**Question 3. You hear a man telling a friend about being unable to study art at school.**
Woman:	Is there a subject you wish you'd taken at school, but didn't?
Man:	Yes, art. We didn't have the option to take that. The focus tended to be on more academic subjects then – you know, science, maths … I'm a bit annoyed about it now. I've always been into painting– not that I ever considered making a living from becoming an artist – I've always wanted to be an engineer … But it would've been useful to learn stuff like knowing how to apply different paints properly when I was younger. I love the skill in those amazing old paintings you can see hanging in galleries.
Narrator:	Now listen again.
Narrator:	**Question 4. You hear two students discussing a sports class they have just attended.**
Boy:	What did you think of that sports class?
Girl:	It made a change from actually *playing* sports, didn't it?
Boy:	Yeah, it did. It was interesting to consider the theoretical side of sport for once – all that detail about the psychology of winning was a new angle on things. Mr Banks is a great teacher. He'd done tons of research, hadn't he?
Girl:	He had. I'm not sure I'll put what we talked about into practice, though. I'm highly unlikely to become a professional athlete.
Boy:	Me neither – though I could see some of the others in the class looked pretty eager to get out there and try some of the techniques.
Narrator:	Now listen again.
Narrator:	**Question 5. You hear a girl telling a friend about her brother.**
Boy:	Hasn't your brother got a place at university?
Girl:	Yes, he has! He's going to study physics.
Boy:	Is he looking forward to it?
Girl:	I think on the whole he's pretty enthusiastic about going on to the next

	step. … I get the impression he isn't quite as confident as I'd have expected him to be about getting to know the others on the course. I don't think it's that he thinks they'll be better than him at the subject or anything like that, but there's something, … maybe it's just nerves. Anyway, once he starts classes, he's going to be so busy with work that I'm sure whatever's bothering him now will fade away.
Narrator:	Now listen again.
Narrator:	**Question 6. You hear a student talking to his teacher about an assignment.**
Boy:	Can I have a word about the English assignment you've set us?
Woman:	Yes, of course you can.
Boy:	We have to write a blog about something which interests us. I don't know much about the ideas you gave us, so would you mind if I did something different?
Woman:	Not at all. The main thing is that you've got some experience of what you're writing about.
Boy:	I do, but I need to do some background reading online. … The other thing is I've never done anything like this, so I don't know how formal the language should be.
Woman:	OK. Let me give you the address of a website which will help.
Boy:	Great, thanks.
Narrator:	Now listen again.
Narrator:	**Question 7. You hear a science teacher talking to her class.**
Woman:	OK, everyone, listen up! Now, I've become aware that there's been a bit of a misunderstanding about where we're holding our science classes while the labs are being repainted. They won't be in the main hall as some of you seem to think, but in the school gym. Obviously, we won't be able to carry out any chemistry experiments or practical work in there, but it's a temporary situation. We'll be able to spend a bit of time on some theory instead. I'm optimistic that this will be a good use of our time as it'll give you the chance to clarify anything you've been having difficulties with in class.
Narrator:	Now listen again.

Narrator:	Question 8. You hear two friends discussing learning foreign languages.
Woman:	A lot of British people can't see the point of learning foreign languages when people in other countries speak English, but I think that shows a lack of understanding.
Man:	Me too. You get more out of a language class than the words themselves – like understanding other countries' way of life, and their history.
Woman:	– and their values, even.
Man:	Exactly. It's true people *do* speak English around the world, so it's not strictly necessary to know other languages, but you get more out of a trip if you know a few words.
Woman:	Yeah, there's a limit to how much you cancommunicatebytryingtoactoutyourideas!
Narrator:	Now listen again.

Listening Part 1:2

1
1 astonishing
2 fascinating
3 entertained
4 irritating
5 exhausted
6 motivated
7 thrilling
8 encouraging

2 1 don't 2 won't 3 haven't 4 aren't

3 1 Who 2 What 3 What 4 How

4 1 A 2 B 3 B 4 B
  5 C 6 C 7 C 8 A

Narrator:	🔊 Track 2 Listening Part 1 Worksheet 2
	You will hear people talking in eight different situations. For questions 1–8, choose the best answer (A, B or C).
Narrator:	Question 1. You hear an announcement about a band called the Big Bang.
Man:	This next piece of local news will be of interest to musicians. Some of you'll have heard of the Big Bang. You may even have been lucky enough to see them play since they started a year ago. If you have, then you'll know what a brilliant folk group they are. Well, now there's an opportunity to meet them in person at their workshops on the first Sunday of the month, where you can learn to play some of their entertaining tunes! Don't

	get your hopes up of joining the band, though – they aren't taking on anyone new at the moment – but why not go along and benefit from their expertise?
Narrator:	Now listen again.
Narrator:	Question 2. You hear a young woman telling her friend about an article she has read.
Woman:	I've just read this article about having hobbies.
Man:	What did it say?
Woman:	Well, although exercise is good for us, there's evidence to suggest that the more you do, the more injuries you suffer. Sounds like a good reason not to worry about only doing a couple of hours a week.
Man:	Interesting!
Woman:	The article mentioned loads of hobbies I'd never heard of. I can't say anything particularly appealed, but there was one other thing ... you know how people go on about not doing too much gaming, don't you? Well, apparently it makes you smarter! So, I'm no longer concerned about my health and I'm going to buy a new game.
Narrator:	Now listen again.
Narrator:	Question 3. You hear two friends discussing free time.
Woman:	It always amazes me how many interests you have. I'd be exhausted!
Man:	I've only got two or three I do regularly. I can't live without sport, but I'm sometimes exhausted afterwards. I often get back home, and just sit down on the sofa for a couple of hours!
Woman:	Well, it's good to have time to empty your mind.
Man:	You're right, I used to pack as much as I could into my time off – I must have tried every hobby there is! But now I need time to chill out.
Woman:	Me too. You don't need to be busy all the time. Getting out of the house for a walk helps me relax sometimes.
Man:	And me.
Narrator:	Now listen again.
Narrator:	Question 4. You hear a boy telling a friend about the sport of diving.
Girl:	You're a diver, aren't you?
Boy:	Yeah. But in a swimming pool – not deep-sea diving.

Girl:	Oh I see – the sort of diving where you jump off a diving board and twist and turn in the air before entering the water? That must be terrifying!
Boy:	I never suffered from nerves, though I can see why standing on the ten-metre board might make some people want to climb back down again! You just have to go for it. There's nothing like knowing you've got it just right – it's incredible, you want to do it like that every time.
Girl:	It's amazing watching really experienced divers do their stuff.
Boy:	I watch them to analyse their moves – it's a different experience when you're a diver yourself!
Narrator:	Now listen again.
Narrator:	**Question 5. You hear two friends talking about hiking.**
Man:	Are you off hiking this weekend?
Woman:	Yeah, I find it very relaxing. It helps to clear my mind.
Man:	I've just joined a walking group myself. I know so little of the surrounding area despite having lived here several years now. I've heard some of the hills round here can be pretty hard going, but I'm sure the exercise won't do me any harm.
Woman:	And there are some fantastic views …
Man:	Mmmm. The truth is I find looking down from heights petrifying. I'm hoping this will cure me of that. If I'm honest, that's my main motivation for giving it a go. Anyway, I'm sure I'll enjoy the views and the fresh air.
Narrator:	Now listen again.
Narrator:	**Question 6. You hear a man telling a friend about producing furniture as a hobby.**
Woman:	Have you got any interesting hobbies?
Man:	Actually, I'm quite passionate about woodwork.
Woman:	That's pretty unusual. What kind of things do you make?
Man:	Small pieces of furniture mainly. I use wood from sustainable sources. Some woodworkers enjoy restoring things, making them look like new. That's not for me. I tend to make stuff that I give away. I don't sell it. I haven't got space in my house, so I don't do it 'cos I need more

	cupboard space or anything. It's just for fun. I find that it helps to balance the dullness of my job where there isn't much room to express myself.
Woman:	Fantastic!
Narrator:	Now listen again.
Narrator:	**Question 7. You hear a review of a film.**
Woman:	This week's film of the week sees Ricky Riley return as the hero in Mark Martin's latest thriller, *Midnight*. I'm sure you all remember Riley's stunning acting in *Red Wood* last year. Well, I'm afraid to say that despite the complex plots and satisfying closing scenes, Riley's performance fails to live up to expectations this time. That isn't to say the film isn't worth seeing – it most certainly is, though I personally would have liked to see some of the beautiful mountains and lakes of the area the film's set in, rather than the inside of the main character's apartment, which is where most of the action takes place.
Narrator:	Now listen again.
Narrator:	**Question 8. You hear two friends talking about taking photos to put on social media websites.**
Woman:	You take loads of photos, don't you? Do you upload onto the InstantPhoto site?
Man:	Yeah, I do. I've got this amazing phone with loads of different apps on it – you can create all kinds of weird and wonderful effects with it – it's brilliant for experimenting with. People do loads of crazy stuff, though I tend to avoid looking closely at pictures posted by mates in case I'm too influenced by them.
Woman:	You've got to start out with a decent photo in the first place, though, haven't you?
Man:	Yeah, it helps. You'll only get either negative feedback or none at all if the composition or lighting are no good – and no one wants that.
Narrator:	Now listen again.

Listening Part 1:3

1a 1 c 2 d 3 b 4 a

1b Students' own answers.

2 1 burn out 3 break a record
2 push yourself 4 warm up

5 get out of breath
6 work out

7 keep in shape
8 do someone good

3 1 C   2 B   3 A   4 B
    5 A   6 A   7 C   8 B

Narrator:	**Track 3 Listening Part 1 Worksheet 3**
	You will hear people talking in eight different situations. For questions 1–8, choose the best answer (A, B or C).
Narrator:	**Question 1. You hear a teacher talking to her class.**
Woman:	I've been talking about the 'walk ten thousands steps a day' programme for a while and I know some of you have already been trying it out, counting your steps with the monitors you've been given. Well done if you've been achieving your daily goal! You can compare how you've been doing with one another, but remember there's no winner. You may think 'what's the point, then?'. Well, it's about keeping in shape. To persuade the rest of you to get going, remember you don't have to go to the sports centre or anything – just keep moving – take the stairs instead of the lift or walk home rather than taking the bus.
Narrator:	Now listen again.
Narrator:	**Question 2. You hear two friends talking about learning to ski.**
Girl:	What do you think of our ski classes?
Boy:	They're great! I've wanted to learn for ages, so I'm keen to push myself as far as I can.
Girl:	Don't you find it exhausting? You need loads of strength to pick yourself up when you fall over – which I don't seem to have.
Boy:	Yes, I suppose you do … but that's not an issue for me – I just can't seem to get the turns right, no matter how hard I try.
Girl:	Nor can I! But I'm sure we'll get it one day. Then we'll have more of a laugh in the class.
Boy:	Yes, I'm looking forward to it!
Narrator:	Now listen again.
Narrator:	**Question 3. You hear a sports instructor talking to an athletics class.**
Man:	Right, who's up for trying to beat the centre's long jump record? For those of you who are interested, we'll be doing

additional practice every Saturday afternoon from one till three. Now, contrary to what some of you might think, it's not a record I set myself, nor have I ever attempted any long jump record – I'm much better suited to high jump, as you know. Anyway, it's quite a while since the current record was set, and though I know you probably think it'll be tricky to beat, with our training facilities and your fitness levels, I see no reason why someone in this group shouldn't be able to do it!

Narrator:	Now listen again.
Narrator:	**Question 4. You hear a girl telling a friend about lessons on eating and exercising that she has done at school.**
Boy:	What have you been doing in school recently?
Girl:	We've been doing loads on health and fitness – about eating and exercising. I was already aware of some of the stuff we talked about – like the importance of a balanced diet. I've always made the effort to eat carbohydrates, like pasta and potatoes, when I'm going to gymnastics classes later, 'cos I know they give you energy. But apparently, you can actually have more than I do 'cos you burn it off. That was news to me. I'm sure what they said was right – but I feel OK with what I've been doing, so I'll just carry on as usual.
Narrator:	Now listen again.
Narrator:	**Question 5. You hear a student talking to his sports teacher about getting fit.**
Woman:	How can I help you, Alex?
Boy:	I wondered if you could give me some advice. I'm really into sports – I love our classes at school but I'd like to push myself further.
Woman:	What did you have in mind?
Man:	Well, I'm into running, as you know, and I wouldn't mind entering some events outside school, to see if I can beat other people my age. I've been trying to build up my strength and stamina on the machines at the gym – I asked a friend of mine to train with me – and now I want to take things to the next level.
Woman:	Let me see what I can find out for you.
Narrator:	Now listen again.

Narrator:	Question 6. You hear two friends talking about a TV programme they have watched.
Man:	I watched this programme about sleep the other night.
Woman:	Oh, yeah, so did I – about the health benefits of getting enough?
Man:	Yeah, that's it. They've done a ton of research into sleep. Did you know that your brain's actually working harder when you're asleep than when you're awake? That was unexpected!
Woman:	Really? I'd heard that previously. If I'm honest, there wasn't an awful lot that was new to me. But I ought to be following the recommendations on how to sleep better. The problem is I forget.
Man:	Stuff like ensuring your bedroom's dark enough, not thinking about the next day's challenges?
Woman:	Exactly. It was good to be reminded about all that.
Narrator:	Now listen again.
Narrator:	Question 7. You hear an expert talking about what being healthy really means.
Woman:	Being healthy isn't just about physical fitness, but psychological well-being too. No matter how well you eat or how much you exercise, if you're burned out from working or studying all the time and don't build in a life beyond this, it won't do you any good. Most of us have listened to the warnings and make time to spend with loved ones and get to the gym. What's failing to get through is what good nutrition means – we know we need certain vitamins for example, but still too many of us take them in tablet form instead of the food which contains them. Better education is the key.
Narrator:	Now listen again.
Narrator:	Question 8. You hear a fitness expert talking about warming up before exercise.
Man:	Part of exercising safely is warming up properly, especially if you're going to do something high energy, like working out in the gym. Yet too many people go straight out there without making sure their muscles are ready for exercise – which results in unnecessary injury – even while knowing this is the incorrect

thing to do. I understand people may have little time to exercise and try to fit it in between work or study and dinner-time, but you need to build up to being slightly out of breath with an increased heart rate before you begin your main exercise session. Finding warm-up activities you like doing will keep you motivated.

Narrator:	Now listen again.

Get it right!
I know you don't like sports. **Neither / Nor** do I.

Listening Part 2:1

1 Noun: catering, chop, portion, taste, vitamin
Verb: chop, consume, swallow, taste
Adjective: balanced, catering

2
1 balanced diet	7 chocolate
2 fuel	8 chewing
3 fat(s)	9 coffee
4 quantities	10 (doing) exercise / (playing) sport(s)
5 recipes	
6 sunlight	

Narrator:	Track 4 Listening Part 2 Worksheet 1 **You will hear a girl called Lydia giving a talk about a project she has been involved in on healthy eating. For questions 1–10, complete the sentences with a word or short phrase. You now have 45 seconds to look at the questions.**
Lydia:	Hi, I'm Lydia and I'm going to tell you about a project I'm involved in about how to have a healthy diet, as part of our health and fitness campaign at school. This is what's otherwise known as maintaining a balanced diet. It's crucial to eat properly in order to decrease the risk of suffering from disease later in life.
	You could say that our body is a machine and that the food we eat is its fuel. Without it – or without the right kinds of it – we'd find it difficult to study or move around without becoming weak and exhausted.
	So, what does healthy eating really mean? Everyone's aware that there are certain foods we ought to avoid and others we should eat plenty of. It isn't a

case of simply avoiding particular food groups altogether, though. Not all fats are bad for us, for example, and living solely on say, fruit and vegetables, could mean cutting out vital nutrients.

What should we be eating, then? Have you seen what I call the food pyramid? It's basically a diagram in the shape of a triangle, with a wide base and a pointed top, and it gives you an idea of what you should eat and in what quantities. It's divided into four layers, with the foods you need most of in the bottom layer, such as potatoes and bread, and those you should have a minimal amount of in the top layer – like oil and sweets. The food triangle's a good place to start if you aren't sure <u>what</u> to cut down or eat more of.

In the middle of the triangle are fruit and vegetables. You've no doubt heard that we should eat five portions of these every day. There are good reasons for eating these – from providing us with much-needed fibre, to protecting us against health problems, like high blood pressure. You can have them as juice, or create soups, if you don't enjoy eating them whole. I've got some recipes I can give you afterwards if anyone wants them. They're delicious. The different vitamins found in fruit and vegetables also have important functions. For example, vitamin A helps us maintain healthy eyesight, and is found in orange vegetables like carrots. Vitamin D, on the other hand, strengthens our bones – it's also produced in our bodies with the help of sunlight, so not only should you try to include it in your diet but get outside often, too.

Now I'm going to talk to you a little about food myths! There are some snacks which we've been told to believe are pretty unhealthy for us. I'm not going to say a packet of crisps is OK – they're fried and covered in salt. But chocolate, you'll be relieved to find out, is not the worst thing you can eat – though large amounts should be avoided, of course. Certain types are actually OK for us – the dark variety contains iron, in fact, which our bodies need for healthy blood.

There's another myth that chewing certain raw salad items, such as celery, consumes more energy than it gives you. People eat lots of it, thinking they're going to lose weight, but I'm sorry to say that this so-called 'fact' simply isn't true!

Turning to drinks, now … It's important not to fill up on fizzy drinks which contain a ton of sugar. And though we tend to think it's really good for us, juice has a lot of sugar, too, so we shouldn't have more than one glass a day. On the other hand, we think we ought to avoid coffee. However, it contains important chemicals which can help us digest our food, by taking what our bodies need from it.

Finally, you hear people saying 'It doesn't matter what I eat as long as I do plenty of exercise'. Well, of course, running or playing sports is great for you – but you shouldn't rely on them as the main way you keep healthy. It's good, fresh food which feeds our brains and bodies.

Narrator: Now listen again.

3a 1 to cut down means to eat or drink less of something
2 to eat up means to finish everything you've been given
3 to heat up means to make warm
4 to live on means to eat only a particular food

3b Students' own answers.

4 Students' own answers.

Listening Part 2:2

1 Responsibility: duty, task
Salary: earnings, income
Job: position, profession
Employ: hire, take on

2 1 festivals
2 jewellery
3 nervous
4 to-do list
5 suppliers
6 satisfying
7 tourism
8 determined
9 backup plan
10 customer service

Narrator: **Track 5 Listening Part 2 Worksheet 2**

You will hear a young woman called Jenny Smythe talking about her job as an events organiser. For questions 1–10, complete the sentences with a word or short phrase. You now have 45 seconds to look at the questions.

Jenny: Hello, my name's Jenny Smythe, and I'm here to tell you about my position as an events organiser, which is exactly what it sounds like – I organise events! That can be anything from exhibitions and conferences, which are interesting, though not terribly exciting, to my personal favourite – festivals. I've also organised things like product launches, too.

At the moment I'm organising a street fair in the town I live in, which has different areas known as quarters. Each one is known for the type of products it produces. In this case the fair's in the jewellery quarter, but there's also an annual fair in the clothing quarter, and the artist's quarter has a yearly event, too.

This is the first time a fair will have taken place in this part of town, so everyone's pretty enthusiastic about it. It should be fun provided that everything goes according to plan. This will be my first ever street fair, and I'd be excited, too, if I wasn't so nervous, though as long as I plan carefully and give myself enough time, everything should go well.

Let me tell you more about my role. Once I take on a job, I need to consider all the tasks that need doing and prioritise them. This means creating what's known as a 'to-do list'. It involves listing everything that needs to be done and setting realistic deadlines. Imagine having a fair and forgetting to organise tables for the stalls, for example!

One of the first things I'll do when I've got an event to organise is discuss things with the client – it's crucial to find out what they have in mind because it's their event, not mine. Then I can start to approach suppliers – the people who will provide everything we need to make sure an event goes smoothly – which can be everything from food to music.

When everything comes together and an event is successful, it's really satisfying to see people enjoying themselves. That's always far more important to me than the income I make doing the job – though, that's nice too, of course! Being thanked for my role in making it happen motivates me to get on with the next job.

People often ask me how I got into events organising. They assume I'll have done a qualification in marketing or event management itself – tourism is what I actually studied, and it's been quite useful in some ways. You can enter the field with any qualification really, as long as you've got the right personality and are prepared to work hard.

So, what skills are needed for the job then? It goes without saying that you need to be organised – and being flexible is helpful too – customers often change their minds about what they want during the planning process. Above all else, I'd say you've got to be determined. Things can and do go wrong when you're planning events and you can't just give up!

Let me give you an example of something that happened to me. It was the morning of an event and I got a call to say the roof was leaking at the hall we were using and it wasn't safe for visitors. This is where what's known as a backup plan is crucial, so I was glad I'd created one in advance! In this instance, I managed to find an alternative venue using my contacts – something you build up over time and which can save you from all kinds of unexpected happenings.

If you're interested in doing this job, either now or in the future, it's a good idea to get some experience first – even if you don't make any money. What I did was work in a hotel, which was great because I learned about dealing with people and sorting out problems. However, work in all types of customer service roles is helpful, and that's what I'd say you should aim to do.

I hope I've inspired some of you to join this fascinating profession. Does anyone have any questions?

Narrator: Now listen again.

3a
1 considering
2 now
3 provided
4 though
5 whereas
6 once
7 where
8 if

3b
1 where
2 provided
3 Considering
4 Now
5 whereas
6 once
7 if
8 though

Listening Part 2:3

1
1 Green
2 Conservation
3 Worldwide
4 Climate change
5 Endangered
6 Pollute
7 Evolution
8 Ecology

2
1 have you been interested in
2 have been clearing
3 has been going on
4 have learned
5 Have / 've just found out
6 Have you ever looked
7 has travelled
8 have / 've been studying

3
1 tiger
2 woodland
3 insects
4 highway
5 tunnel
6 leaves
7 climbing skills
8 rescue centre
9 pets
10 Wildlife Trust

Narrator:	**Track 6 Listening Part 2 Worksheet 3**
	You will hear a boy called Jake Castle giving a class presentation about an animal called a hedgehog. For questions 1–10, complete the sentences with a word or short phrase. You now have 45 seconds to look at the questions.
Jake:	We've been asked to talk about something we do outside school which helps the environment in some way, and I've decided to talk about the hedgehog conservation work I've been doing recently with a local conservation club.
	There's been a huge decline in hedgehog numbers over recent years. In case you don't know what a hedgehog looks like – it's a four-legged creature not dissimilar in size to a small rabbit – with a long nose and it's covered in sharp spikes. Depending on where you live, you may have seen one before. Though, since they're

disappearing at the same rate as the tiger, it's quite likely you haven't. What's the reason for the rapid decrease in the hedgehog population in the UK? Like many threatened animals, the problem is its habitat is disappearing. Hedgehogs live not only in the countryside, but in woodland, too. As these environments disappear to make way for housing or intensive agriculture, so do the hedgehogs.

As the hedgehog's habitat is destroyed, so is their food source. Hedgehogs have a pretty big appetite, and a single animal can eat over a hundred smaller creatures every night! Worms are a favourite snack, as are insects and other little animals, so we need to protect these, too.

Let me tell you about some of the things that can be done to help save the hedgehog population. One thing we're promoting at the club is what we call the hedgehog highway, which doesn't mean building a special bridge or road for them – though that would be cool – but making sure they can pass from garden to garden without obstacles getting in the way. This means cutting holes in the fences between gardens. These don't have to be big and neighbours can get together to help each other out. Alternatives include digging a tunnel under a wall or whatever else is in the way. These measures allow hedgehogs to walk from garden to garden in search of food and shelter.

Speaking of shelter, it's becoming increasingly difficult for hedgehogs to find suitable places to build nests. It's crucial for them to have a safe place to hide and sleep during colder months when they hibernate. So, we're encouraging people to think twice before you clear away leaves and, instead pile them up with branches in quiet corners of the garden to create the perfect cosy hedgehog home.

You may be surprised to learn that since they don't possess brilliant eyesight, hedgehogs have a tendency to fall into things like ponds or drains, so it's crucial that people cover these dangers wherever they can. I've placed small stacks of stones at the side of the pond in my parents' garden so they can get out – their climbing skills are surprisingly strong, I discovered.

I've come across several injured hedgehogs while I've been working with the conservation club, and it's vital to know what should be done when this happens. Vets can help injured hedgehogs – the preferred course of action, though, is to go online and find out where the nearest rescue centre is – and take them there.

Hedgehogs do wake up to eat during their hibernation period in winter, and we're asking neighbours that do see one out and about in their garden to have a look and check it doesn't seem underweight. If it's a bit thin, there's no problem with leaving some food out for it. Bread may seem like something easy to leave, but it's impossible for hedgehogs to digest it, so I'd recommend food usually given to pets instead.

I hope some of you will go out and start looking after hedgehogs. If they're not found in your area and you still want to get involved in the conservation of other species, there's plenty you can do. The club I'm in is called the Green Trust, but the Wildlife Trust is a fantastic place to start if you want to find out more about what's happening with other animals in your local area. You can easily find them online, but I can give you the website address if you like.

I hope I've inspired you ...

Narrator: Now listen again.

Get it right!
Since the end of the Second World War, the world's population **has been** increasing / has increased rapidly.

Listening Part 3:1

1a
1 b	2 h	3 f	4 d
5 g	6 a	7 c	8 e

1b
1 make a purchase
2 debit card
3 designer clothing
4 find a bargain
5 casually-dressed
6 be out of stock
7 browse the internet
8 launch a new range

2 1 G 2 F 3 E 4 B 5 D

Narrator: Track 7 Listening Part 3 Worksheet 1

You will hear five short extracts in which people are talking about shopping for clothes. For questions 1–5, choose from the list (A–H), what each speaker enjoys about shopping for clothes. Use the letters only once. There are three extra letters which you do not need to use. You now have 30 seconds to look at the questions.

Narrator: Speaker 1

Man: I'm a fashion model, so you might expect me to be really into clothes. Actually, I couldn't care less about them, especially when I've been taking them on and off all day at work. Designer gear's not my style – though I do try a ton of it on when I'm at a photo shoot. Having said that, it isn't that I've no interest in shopping at all – as long as it isn't for myself. Working in fashion, I have a pretty good eye for what'll look good on my sisters, so if I'm out and about and spot something in a shop, it'll often end up going home to them.

Narrator: Speaker 2

Girl: My friends are forever dragging me out shopping. I pretend I'm not into it, but there's something satisfying about spotting a dress or top in a high-street store that's similar in design to one you've seen in a magazine for ten times the price. Not that the high-street versions are always cheap, but it's still a good feeling. We usually pop in and see one of our friends who works in a store we like. We always beg her for money off anything we buy, but she doesn't have the authority to give us discounts. So, I'm not the most fashionable person around, but I try to look my best.

Narrator: Speaker 3

Boy: Well, I don't have money of my own so I tend to go shopping with my dad. He told me he doesn't mind what I get as long as it doesn't cost a fortune. So designer stuff's out – though now and then I'll see if I can get him to let me put something weird and wonderful on just to have a laugh. Otherwise, shopping's really not that cool, is it? Dad's really into the latest trends, though, and he's always saying

'What do you reckon about this T-shirt – does it go with these jeans?', stuff like that. You'd expect it to be the other way round really, wouldn't you?

Narrator: **Speaker 4**

Girl: I work in a clothes shop – not because I've ever been particularly into fashion, I just needed a job! Contrary to what you might think, in this store sales assistants can't buy things cheaper, though now and then the manager will let us choose something that's slightly damaged. Most of the time you wouldn't know it's not perfect – there might be a button missing or something, but there's always a spare. Part of my job is to dress the window displays that people see as they walk past the shop – and this is something that I now love looking out for when I'm out shopping myself.

Narrator: **Speaker 5**

Man: I've never done much online shopping, certainly not for clothes. Mainly, 'cos I can't be bothered to send stuff back that doesn't fit or whatever. And when you like to treat yourself now and then to something pretty special, you want to make sure it's OK. I'm not into the wacky stuff some of the designers produce – you can't walk down the street dressed like that – and being on-trend isn't a major concern of mine. I prefer their more classic pieces that will stand the test of time, so I keep an eye out for their sales. I wouldn't call myself a bargain hunter and I don't buy much, either.

Narrator: Now listen again.

---

3 1 I'd worn
2 used to be
3 Have
4 was standing
5 was already waiting
6 been browsing
7 was
8 You've been

Listening Part 3:2

1 1 estate
2 lobby
3 basement
4 cellar; cellar and basement are similar in meaning
5 corridor
6 property
7 studio
8 terrace

2 1 H 2 D 3 B 4 F 5 G

Narrator: **Track 8 Listening Part 3 Worksheet 2**

You will hear five short extracts in which people are talking about houses they used to live in. For questions 1–5, choose from the list (A–H) the main disadvantage of each speaker's previous house. Use the letters only once. There are three extra letters which you do not need to use. You now have 30 seconds to look at the questions.

Narrator: **Speaker 1**

Woman: Although we used to live in an old farmhouse, you could hardly say it was peaceful in the countryside – there was always something going on – animals, tractors … . I miss that now we've moved into town. But at least here you can move from room to room freely – in our old house the upstairs rooms were linked so you had to pass through each one to get to the next. It was really odd the way it had been altered like that.

I'm slowly getting used to being in town – it's more convenient, though and we look out over a park, which reminds me of the place we left.

Narrator: **Speaker 2**

Man: My wife and I bought this huge old house after we first got married with the intention of doing it up and selling it on at a profit. Of course, like all good intentions it didn't quite happen that way. We ended up pouring more and more time into just making essential repairs and never got the rest to the standard we'd have liked. The layout was its best feature and we brought all our kids up there. They used to have great fun running around in the basement shouting their heads off. Now they've left home, we've downsized to a modern flat where everything's in top condition – that's great.

Narrator: **Speaker 3**

Girl: I lived in an old house till we moved last year, when I turned fifteen, and needed my own space. I used to share with my sister. We didn't always get on with each other and we often used to argue, so I'm glad I've got my own room now. The other thing I didn't mind getting away from was the cold air that used to come through the windows 'cos they didn't close properly. We had to pull the blankets right up round our ears to keep cosy in winter. I liked the house, and though we didn't know our neighbours, it was a nice place to grow up.

Narrator: Speaker 4

Boy: We moved to the city from the countryside a couple of years ago and though I've never really got used to the noise, I wouldn't say I miss being in the middle of nowhere. If I wanted to see my mates I'd have to cycle kilometres – often in the rain. Now I can see them any time I want. There's not much to look at out of the windows in the place I live now, apart from other buildings, but I've got a massive room and that suits me. It's a bit of a weird design this house – my bedroom's on the ground floor, but it's not really a problem.

Narrator: Speaker 5

Woman: Our new place is a bit cramped, so sometimes it doesn't feel like there's enough space for us all, but it's only temporary till we move to Spain. And we're saving money by not renting something bigger. For the moment we've got a fantastic terrace on the roof – I go up there whenever I'm in need of a bit of fresh air. In that way it's better than our old place. There are also no huge trees overshadowing our garden and no arguments with the people next door about them! That sort of thing is always a drawback of living so close to others. But there's no such problem here.

Narrator: Now listen again.

3a 1 used to
2 use to
3 used to
4 didn't use
5 getting used to
6 are used to / have got used to
7 Didn't / Did
8 got used to

3b 1 c   2 b   3 a

3c Students' own answers.

Listening Part 3:3

1a 1 relieved
2 amused
3 impressed
4 fed up
5 cheerful
6 puzzled
7 enthusiastic
8 dissatisfied

1b Student's own answers.

2 1 C   2 A   3 F   4 D   5 B

Narrator: **Track 9 Listening Part 3 Worksheet 3**

You will hear five short extracts in which people are talking about holiday accommodation. For questions 1–5, choose from the list (A–H) each speaker's first impression of the accommodation. Use the letters only once. There are three extra letters which you do not need to use. You now have 30 seconds to look at the questions.

Narrator: Speaker 1

Woman: When we arrived at the holiday villa we were renting in Spain, we were thrilled with it. We'd flown over some spectacular mountains on the way in and, even though the land wasn't so high where the house was, when we had our first glimpse of it sitting there on the hill, we thought it was breathtaking. You wouldn't call it beautiful – it was a bit too rocky and treeless – but the way it was situated certainly made an impact. One disadvantage was that there were no shops nearby. Despite that it wasn't quiet – there was a lot of agricultural work going on in the fields.

Narrator: Speaker 2

Boy: We stayed in this amazing hotel in Italy last year. It was my family's first time abroad and my sister and I were excited about it. We knew the hotel was in this village so we were expecting it to be quiet. But, actually, we got to know loads of people our age when we hung out.
It took half an hour to walk from one side of the hotel to the other! OK, I'm exaggerating, but when we arrived we were like, 'Wow, this place is huge!' The rooms were pretty good – though, in the picture online it showed them with cool TVs and there wasn't one in mine.

Narrator: Speaker 3

Woman: A group of us rented an apartment in Mexico last summer. We'd spent ages searching for just the right thing with enough bedrooms and outside space. When we opened the door after an exhausting journey, nothing could have prepared us for how luxurious it felt – the photos certainly didn't match up to how lovely it was. I slept incredibly well in my cosy bed. There could have been a few more home comforts – a hairdryer or kitchen stuff, and while our neighbours in the apartment next door were friendly, we didn't see much of anyone else around. That was probably a good job – we were rather noisy at times!

Narrator: **Speaker 4**

Boy: I love camping and my dad and I go every school holiday. We've got all our own gear, but this one time we decided to go to this awesome campsite where everything's already set up for you. As soon as we walked in we were like, 'Yeah, this is exactly what we wanted!' – a really cool spot right on the lakeside where you could go swimming – perfect for us! We still should have taken some stuff – there weren't many cooking utensils and it was pretty basic. I'm not usually bothered when places are a bit noisy – I didn't expect to be kept awake half the night by other people's music, though.

Narrator: **Speaker 5**

Woman: We were really impressed by the cottage we rented out on holiday a couple of weeks ago. We didn't know a lot about the area, though it looked stunning on the website. It was nice – I think the website photographer must have used some interesting angles to get those particular shots, though! What was immediately remarkable was the silence – I slept like a baby! The only thing we felt let down by was nobody coming to meet us when we arrived – we'd expected the owners to be there. They'd sounded really friendly when we arranged the accommodation on the phone, so that was strange. Anyway, we had a great time.

Narrator: Now listen again.

3a
1 Terminal
2 boarded
3 aircraft
4 take-off
5 captain
6 approach
7 landing
8 scheduled

3b
1 scheduled
2 captain
3 approach
4 board
5 take-off
6 aircraft
7 landing
8 terminal

Get it right!
Our holiday was very amusing, and Crete was beautiful.

Listening Part 4:1

1
1 manners
2 interpret
3 values
4 tradition
5 dress
6 beliefs
7 culture shock
8 diverse

2
1 patiently
2 brilliantly
3 eagerly
4 warmly
5 curiously
6 accidentally
7 nervously
8 enthusiastically

3 1 A   2 B   3 A   4 B   5 C   6 C   7 C

Narrator: 🔊 **Track 10 Listening Part 4, Worksheet 1**
You will hear an interview with a travel writer called Anna Bryant, who is talking about what to do when visiting other countries. For questions 1–7, choose the best answer (A, B or C). You now have one minute to look at the questions.

Man: Good morning Anna, and thank you for joining us on the Travel Programme. You're here to talk about travelling to other countries and how to deal with cultural differences. How can you find out about a country's culture before you travel?

Anna: Well, it's often tempting to turn to guide books, though many focus on things to do rather than how to behave. If you're lucky enough to know someone from the country you're visiting – I rarely have been – you've got the perfect consultant! My preference is to eat in a restaurant where the staff are from the place you're planning to visit – you can observe things like greetings and table manners. That isn't always possible, either, but it's worth a try!

Man: How can you get over the language barrier?

Anna: It does no harm to try to use the local language, especially if it's one you've studied at school. Even if you only remember a bit it helps – though maybe, not much! Often, you might not know any of the language and you'll have to rely on hand gestures or even drawing. I've been in situations where nobody understood a word anyone else was saying. Surprisingly the messages got across and now that's the least of my concerns when travelling, though I try to pick up as much language as I can.

Man:	One thing people worry about is how to behave when visiting someone in their home.
Anna:	Some people are concerned that telling their host they're nervous is rude – personally, I see little wrong with explaining why that's the case. It provides the host with the opportunity to make you feel at home. Otherwise, you could be trying to do what they're doing and get confused – copying them means you could end up behaving like the host instead of the guest. Talking to other people before you go might help, but every family has its own particular traditions, so it may not.
Man:	Have you ever made a cultural mistake yourself?
Anna:	Oh, yes, though thankfully I was fortunate enough to have an understanding host who put me at ease, and because of that I'm able to laugh about it now. I don't know why I made the mistake – I took an unlucky number of flowers as a gift. Looking back, it wasn't so serious really – I'd just misunderstood what someone had told me before I went. I'd never make the same mistake again, though.
Man:	Have you ever experienced culture shock?
Anna:	When I've lived abroad, yes. At first everything's exciting, but if you stay longer, you notice differences in cultural values and beliefs, and that can be confusing. Making good friends in a new place takes time, and it's important to try to let things happen rather than desperately trying to do everything at once. Doing familiar things helps – sleeping regular hours and eating food you like. It really worked in helping me get used to my new environment.
Man:	What's the most interesting tradition you've experienced?
Anna:	I remember being in China at New Year and seeing the Lantern Festival – there was this amazing parade of handmade lanterns. Seeing it taught me that no matter how much you think you know about something in advance, it can still take you by surprise! I was desperate to join in but didn't have my own lantern – it was still enormous fun to watch. The images of it are stuck in my memory – I

	needn't worry about forgetting anything, despite not taking any photos.
Man:	Finally, Anna, you're writing a book about culture.
Anna:	That's right. I'm still at the beginning of the process, even though I've been working on it for a while. People who know me keep asking 'Isn't it finished yet?' but you've got to do the preparation. I'm still undecided about whether people will want to read about my own travels, or whether I should just focus on describing customs from around the world. I won't show anyone what I've written till it's finished – I'm hopeful that people will enjoy it!
Narrator:	Now listen again.

Listening Part 4:2

1 1 environmentally friendly
2 carbon footprint
3 atmosphere
4 clean up
5 chemical
6 threaten
7 global warming
8 organic

2 1 B   2 B   3 A   4 B   5 C   6 B   7 A

Narrator:	**Track 11 Listening Part 4 Worksheet 2** **You will hear an interview with a boy called Liam Banks, who helped to organise a local environmental project called a clean-up day. For questions 1–7, choose the best answer (A, B or C). You now have one minute to look at the questions.**
Woman:	Now we're going to talk to a young man called Liam Banks who's here to talk about a 'clean-up' day he helped to organise in his town. Liam, what is a clean-up day and how did you get involved?
Liam:	A clean-up day is where everyone comes together in a town or neighbourhood as volunteers and basically cleans it up, making it tidier and more environmentally friendly. It's easy to think 'that's not my responsibility' and turn away, counting on the local council to deal with it instead. But having gone into various environmental issues in science

classes, I realised we've got a shared responsibility to face up to things and make our communities greener.

Woman: What did you organise for the day?

Liam: I was responsible for getting volunteers together. I was confident I could get a sufficient number of people interested in helping out if I spoke to people – I had tons of convincing arguments! The problem was I couldn't speak to everyone face to face. In the end we got loads of posters printed asking people to just turn up on the day and bring whatever cleaning stuff they had – rubbish sacks, brushes and things like that.

Woman: So, what happened on the day?

Liam: We started early in the morning. Our meeting point was outside the park gates. Everyone was there with buckets and gloves, ready to get on with the work. I was just filled with pride. It was fantastic to see how much people cared about their community. There were a couple of reporters there from local newspapers, too. It hadn't crossed my mind to invite them – one of the other organisers had, though, and they published an article about what we'd done.

Woman: And you cleared the pond out first?

Liam: Yeah – it's not deep, so we got in there and cleared away tons of plastic bags, as well as weeds that were killing off other green plants. There are ducks and fish in the pond and it's crucial for them to have a healthy place to live. When I was in there, I suddenly got annoyed about how the pond had got in such a bad state – there are litter bins everywhere and it's not hard to use them. One thing I learned was that we'll have to make an effort to keep the pond in good condition.

Woman: What else did you do on the day? Were there any disappointments or did everything go well?

Liam: We picked up litter in the centre of town, brushed paths and cleaned the windows of buildings which are currently empty. We got to chat to everyone who'd turned up, even though it was only briefly. One thing we regret is failing to provide refreshments for them – we should have thought of that. Nobody expressed any dissatisfaction with what they had to do, though, or tried to get out of working hard, and I'm really grateful for that.

Woman: How do you feel now about being involved in the clean-up day?

Liam: What we did was just a tiny drop in the ocean – you've got to constantly work hard to get the message out there to people that we need to keep our planet clean and green, not only for our generation but for those to follow. I won't stop here – I've come up with loads of ideas I want to get on with. I know one person can't change the world – but you have to keep shouting about what you believe in and hope other people will back you up.

Woman: How can people be more environmentally friendly?

Liam: Everyone's got busy lives and you can't expect people to give up all their free time to help out in local clean-up operations all the time. But everyone's read articles about people's impact on the Earth and what they can do to minimise damage. There's nothing to stop you turning off the tap while you clean your teeth instead of leaving it running, or making sure you recycle things wherever you can. These things don't really take any time or effort.

Narrator: Now listen again.

3 1 with   2 up   3 in   4 with
5 on   6 with   7 up

Listening Part 4:3

1 1 referee   5 opponent
2 penalty   6 tackle
3 defender   7 pitch
4 division   8 save
football, hockey, lacrosse, rugby (and Students' own ideas)

2 1 B   2 A   3 A   4 C   5 B   6 C   7 A

Narrator: **Track 12 Listening Part 4 Worksheet 3**
You will hear an interview with a springboard diver called Max Hart, who is talking about his sport. For questions 1–7, choose the best answer (A, B or C). You now have one minute to look at the questions.

Woman:	Talking to us today is fourteen-year-old Max Hart, who is a springboard diver. Max, what does this mean?
Max:	Well, it means I jump from high boards into a deep swimming pool and I'm given a score for the way I do it. It's a competitive sport and I've been involved in it since I was about ten. It was a simple progression from doing gymnastics. I loved that – though I never qualified for any competitions – but I thought the two sports were close enough that I could easily take up diving and perhaps qualify in that. I'm quite competitive as my coach will tell you. So, yeah, it seemed the right thing to do.
Woman:	And your first competition was the regional championships.
Max:	Yeah. People assume I must have been pretty anxious about it cos of the other participants, who'd been competing far longer than me. My coach actually commented on how chilled out I was. There was no chance of winning, so I knew I could just have a good time. I still did my best and though not as many people turned up to watch as I'd expected, I still enjoyed hearing people clap my first competitive dive! That was good enough for me.
Woman:	There are lots of different kinds of dive, aren't there?
Max:	Yeah – with interesting names like 'pikes' and 'tucks'. The kind I struggled with initially because of balance were the arm stand dives – the starting position is upside down standing on your hands! I've actually won some competitions doing arm stand dives – and while they're hardly my favourite, I don't avoid doing them 'cos I seem to have gained a decent level of skill in them.
Woman:	I believe you once had to change a competition dive at the last minute?
Max:	Yeah, that was scary! My coach and I realised we'd missed something out that was an essential element of the dive, so we came up with a new one the day before the competition. I'm a quick learner, so it wasn't forgetting what to do that bothered me but the fact that it involved a position my body just won't go into! No amount of practice seems to have made that easier to do for some

	reason. The dive went OK but I didn't enjoy the experience.
Woman:	Do you enjoy your training sessions?
Max:	They're pretty tough as you can imagine – when you land badly in the water it hurts! And there's no question of having a laugh with your classmates – it's serious stuff and there isn't enough time to waste hanging around chatting. I don't have the chance to watch how the others are progressing either – it's all about perfecting my own dives. Putting as much effort in as you can pays off. And even though the advances are small, they're always there.
Woman:	What's next for you? The Olympics?
Max:	Well, the Olympics is one of the greatest events any athlete can enter, but I'm giving it a miss this time round because I've not reached that standard yet. Maybe next time. No, my main ambition is simply to get higher marks for difficulty than I've achieved so far. I need to try some trickier dives. At some point diving in a pair might be worth a try – I haven't come to a decision about that yet.
Woman:	Finally, what do you like most about this sport?
Max:	Good question. You never know how long it'll last – you could have an injury or stop progressing – so far that hasn't happened, thankfully. They always say it's not the winning but the taking part that matters, and that's the way it is for me. When I stand on the platform ready to dive, that's where the real buzz comes in for me. You know everyone's willing you to do well, and there's an energy in the air I don't get anywhere else in life.
Narrator:	Now listen again.

3
1 too much
2 good enough
3 too
4 enough
5 hard enough
6 good enough
7 too
8 too fast

Get it right!
I don't think it's **big enough**.
I think it's possible to go by bike, but we don't have **enough time**.

Speaking Part 1:1

1a
1 look like; b
2 like; d,
3 like; a,
4 alike; c

1b   Students' own answers.

2a   1 d   2 a   3 e   4 c   5 f   6 g   7 b

2b   What?

3a   1 Do you have a small / large or large / small family?
     2 Who are the most important people in your life?
     3 How do you spend time with your family?
     4 Tell us about one of your good friends.
     5 Do you and your family share similar interests?
     6 What do you and your friends enjoy doing together?
     7 Do you and your friends have similar ideas about life?
     8 Who do you get on with best / get on best with in your family?

Narrator:	🔊 Track 13 Speaking Part 1, Worksheet 1
Examiner:	Good morning. My name is Alison Thorn and this is my colleague Daniel Jones. And your names are?
Petra:	Petra Nováková.
Julio:	Julio Fernández.
Examiner:	Can I have your mark sheets, please? Thank you. Where are you from, Petra?
Petra:	I'm from the Czech Republic.
Examiner:	And you, Julio?
Julio:	I'm from Spain.
Examiner:	First we'd like to know something about you. Do you have a large or small family? Who are the most important people in your life? How do you spend time with your family? Tell us about one of your good friends. Do you and your family share similar interests? What do you and your friends enjoy doing together? Do you and your friends have similar ideas about life? Who do you get on with best in your family?

3b   Students' own answers.

Speaking Part 1:2

1   Giving reasons: as / because / since; Obviously, it's …; The main thing is (that) …; The reason for this is (that) …

Adding reasons: Another thing is (that) …; Apart from that …; As well as that …; There's also the fact that …

2   1 Due to the fact   5 so
     2 Since   6 due to
     3 because of   7 therefore
     4 owing to   8 as a result

3a   1 f   2 d   3 b   4 h
     5 e   6 a   7 g   8 c

Narrator:	🔊 Track 14 Speaking Part 1 Worksheet 2
Examiner:	Good morning. My name is Alison Thorn and this is my colleague Daniel Jones. And your names are?
Ben:	Ben Hollande.
Kasia:	Kasia Antek.
Examiner:	Can I have your mark sheets, please? Thank you. Where are you from, Ben?
Ben:	I'm from France.
Examiner:	And you, Kasia?
Kasia:	I'm from Poland.
Examiner:	First we'd like to know something about you. How do you like to spend your evenings and weekends? Do you prefer spending your free time indoors or outdoors? What's your most interesting hobby? What kinds of books or films do you like? Do you enjoy going to the cinema, theatre or concerts? Do you enjoy keeping up with the news? How much do you enjoy parties or large social events? Tell us about something interesting you've done in your free time recently.

3b   Students' own answers.

Speaking Part 1:3

1a   1 d   2 c   3 a   4 b

1b   Students' own answers.

2a   1 ambitions   5 physically
     2 subject   6 environment
     3 on your own   7 online
     4 kind   8 project

Narrator: **Track 15 Speaking Part 1 Worksheet 3**

Examiner: Good morning. My name is Alison Thorn and this is my colleague Daniel Jones. And your names are?

Christina: Christina Schulman.

Juan: Juan Pérez.

Examiner: Can I have your mark sheets, please? Thank you. Where are you from, Christina?

Christina: I'm from Germany.

Examiner: And you, Juan?

Juan: I'm from Mexico.

Examiner: First we'd like to know something about you.

What are your work or study ambitions?

Tell us about the subject which you find most interesting.

Do you prefer working or studying on your own or with other people?

What kind of work would you like to do in the future?

Do you prefer mentally or physically challenging work?

What kind of environment do you enjoy working or studying in?

How often do you go online to find out about something?

Tell us about an interesting work or study project you've done recently.

2b Students' own answers.

3 'd like, 'm planning to, hope that, expect to, want to, intend to, 'm going to, wish

Get it right!
I **hope I** / **'d like to** become a teacher one day. After I graduate, of course!

Speaking Part 2:1

1 1 main similarity
2 both
3 most obvious difference
4 whereas / while
5 nearly as nice as
6 In contrast
7 while / whereas
8 In the same way

2 1 could / may / might
2 could / may / might
3 must
4 can't have
5 could / may / might
6 couldn't have
7 might have
8 must

3 Students' own answers.

Narrator: **Track 16 Speaking Part 2 Worksheet 1**

Examiner: In this part of the test, I'm going to give each of you two photographs. I'd like you to talk about your photographs on your own for about a minute, and also to answer a question about your partner's photographs.

Petra, it's your turn first. Here are your photographs. They show people shopping in different ways.

I'd like you to compare the photographs, and say what the advantages are for the people of shopping in these different ways. All right?

Examiner: Thank you. Julio, do you like shopping online? Why? Why not?

Examiner: Thank you. Can I have the booklet, please?

Now, Julio, here are your photographs. They show people shopping for food in different places. I'd like you to compare the photographs, and say what the people might enjoy about shopping for food in these places. All right?

Examiner: Thank you. Petra, which of these places would you prefer to shop in? Why?

Examiner: Thank you. Can I have the booklet, please?

Speaking Part 2:2

1a Comparing: as with, like, likewise
Contrasting: alternatively, instead of, unlike
Adding: also, as well, what's more

1b Students' own answers.

2 1 d 2 h 3 a 4 c 5 g 6 e 7 b 8 f

3 Students' own answers.

Narrator: **Track 17 Speaking Part 2 Worksheet 2**

Examiner: In this part of the test, I'm going to give each of you two photographs. I'd like you to talk about your photographs on your own for about a minute, and also to answer a question about your partner's photographs. Kasia, it's your turn first. Here are your photographs. They show people doing different water sports. I'd like you to compare the photographs, and say what you think might attract the people to these activities. All right?

Examiner: Thank you. Ben, which of these activities would you most like to do? Why?

Examiner: Thank you. Can I have the booklet, please? Now, Ben, here are your photographs. They show people doing different activities. I'd like you to compare the photographs, and say what the people might find difficult about doing these activities. All right?

Examiner: Thank you. Kasia, what would you like to be able to do? Why?

Examiner: Thank you. Can I have the booklet, please?

Speaking Part 2:3

1 1 far more
2 nowhere near as
3 doesn't look as
4 the more annoyed
5 isn't quite as
6 much later than

2a 1 looks as if
2 seems
3 appear to be
4 looks

2b Students' own answers.

3 Students' own answers.

Narrator: 🔊 **Track 18 Speaking Part 2 Worksheet 3**

Examiner: In this part of the test, I'm going to give each of you two photographs. I'd like you to talk about your photographs on your own for about a minute, and also to answer a question about your partner's photographs. Juan, it's your turn first. Here are your photographs. They show families having different kinds of holidays. I'd like you to compare the photographs, and say why these families might have chosen these different holidays. All right?

Examiner: Thank you. Christina, which of these holidays would you prefer? Why?

Examiner: Thank you. Can I have the booklet, please? Now, Christina, here are your photographs. They show people sightseeing in different ways. I'd like you to compare the photographs, and say what you think the people enjoy about sightseeing in these ways. All right?

Examiner: Thank you. Juan, do you enjoy guided tours? Why? Why not?

Examiner: Thank you. Can I have the booklet, please?

Get it right!

She looks **like** a shy young girl.

Speaking Part 3/4:1

1 Students' own answers.

2 1 h 2 d 3 e 4 a 5 g 6 b 7 f 8 c
and Students' own answers.

3 Students' own answers.

Narrator: 🔊 **Track 19 Speaking Parts 3 and 4 Worksheet 1**

Part 3

Examiner: Now, I'd like you to talk about something together for about two minutes. Here are some things that schools and workplaces do to encourage their students and employees to be healthier and a question for you to discuss. First you have some time to look at the task.

Examiner: Now, talk to each other about why these might be good ways of encouraging students or employees to be healthier.

Examiner: Thank you. Now you have about a minute to decide which way of encouraging students or employees to be healthier would make the most difference to them.

Examiner: Thank you. Can I have the booklet, please?

---

4 Students' own answers.

Narrator: 🔊 **Track 20**
Part 4

Examiner: Do you think you need to join a gym or exercise class in order to get fit? Why?

Some people say that it can be difficult to find time to exercise or cook. What do you think?

Do you agree that you have to spend a lot of money in order to be fit and healthy? Why? Why not?

Apart from exercising and eating well, what else can you do to stay healthy?

How important do you think it is to choose a form of exercise that you enjoy? Why? Why not?

What could you say to encourage someone who doesn't enjoy exercise or healthy food?

Do you think eating meals at regular times helps you stay healthy? Why? Why not?

How important do you think it is to spend some time outdoors every day? Why?

Thank you. That is the end of the test.

Speaking Part 3/4:2

1a Giving an opinion: As far as I'm concerned …, In my experience …, Personally, I'd say that …, Speaking for myself, …

Clarifying an opinion: Let me explain …, The reason I say this is because …, To put it another way …, What I mean by that is …

1b Students' own answers.

2 1 c 2 f 3 b 4 g 5 e 6 a 7 h 8 d

3 Students' own answers.

Narrator: 🔊	**Track 21 Speaking Parts 3 and 4 Worksheet 2**
	Part 3
Examiner:	Now, I'd like you to talk about something together for about two minutes. Here are some activities that families with teenage children can do together and a question for you to discuss. First you have some time to look at the task.
Examiner:	Now, talk to each other about the advantages and disadvantages for families with teenage children of doing these activities together.
Examiner:	Thank you. Now you have about a minute to decide which activity you think is best for bringing families with teenage children closer together.
Examiner:	Thank you. Can I have the booklet, please?

4 Students' own answers.

Narrator: 🔊	**Track 22**
	Part 4
Examiner:	How important is it for people to spend time with friends rather than family? Why?
	Would you agree that it's important to spend time with friends individually rather than in a group? Why? Why not?
	Do you think eating together helps families get along well? Why?

Do you think it's important for friends to share the same values? Why? Why not?

Thank you. That is the end of the test.

Speaking Part 3/4:3

1 Agreement: I couldn't agree more (very strong), No doubt about it (very strong), I agree to a large extent (quite strong), I partly agree (not very strong)
Disagreement: I'm not sure about that (not very strong), I'd say the exact opposite (very strong), I totally disagree (very strong), No way (very strong)

2 Students' own answers.

3a
1 balance	5 hand
2 whole	6 Although
3 tend	7 sides
4 general	8 account

3b to present a balanced argument; students' own answers.

4 Students' own answers.

Narrator: 🔊	**Track 23 Speaking Parts 3 and 4 Worksheet 3**
Examiner:	Now, I'd like you to talk about something together for about two minutes. Here are some activities that people learning English can do to improve their speaking skills and a question for you to discuss. First you have some time to look at the task.
Examiner:	Now talk to each other about how these activities might help people learning English to improve their speaking skills.
Examiner:	Thank you. Now you have about a minute to decide which activity would be least helpful to people learning English.
Examiner:	Thank you. Can I have the booklet, please?

5 Students' own answers.

Narrator: 🔊	**Track 24**
	Part 4
Examiner:	What do you think the most important school subjects are?
	What else do you think children should be taught in school?
	Do you think there are some things you can't learn at school? What kinds of things?

How important do you think it is to include physical exercise at school? Why?

How important do you think academic qualifications are? Why?

Some people say it is impossible to get a good job without a university degree. Do you agree? Why? Why not?

Do you think TV can be a good educational tool? Why? Why not?

Some people say that you shouldn't trust what you read on the internet. Do you agree?

Thank you. That is the end of the test.

Get it right!

I think you **will agree** with me.

Think about it
Reading and Use of English Part 1

1 True
2 False (there are four options)
3 True
4 True
5 False (only one answer is correct)
6 False (there are eight questions)
7 True
8 False (it is about 160 words long)

Reading and Use of English Part 2

1 grammar	5 word
2 linkers	6 160
3 eight	7 topics
4 example	8 vocabulary

Reading and Use of English Part 3

1 160	5 word
2 word formation	6 spelling
3 eight	7 prefixes
4 filling in a gap	8 two changes

Reading and Use of English Part 4

1 True
2 False (they are about a variety of topics)
3 True
4 False (you complete six sentences)
5 True
6 True
7 False (you must use the word exactly as it is given)
8 False (you must complete the gap with between two and five words, including the key word)

Reading and Use of English Part 5

1 g   2 f   3 d   4 e   5 h   6 a   7 b   8 c

Reading and Use of English Part 6

1 articles	5 does not fit
2 answer options	6 more than one
3 have been removed	7 individual sentences
4 numbered gap	8 signalling and linking

Reading and Use of English Part 7

1 True   2 True   3 True
4 False (there may be more than one question for each text)
5 False (there are ten questions in this part of the exam)
6 True   7 True   8 True

Writing Part 1

1 an essay
2 two
3 must
4 190
5 is
6 should
7 paragraphs
8 a conclusion and your opinion

Writing Part 2

1 True
2 False (you cannot choose an essay in Part 2)
3 True
4 False (all the tasks specify the same word count of 140–190 words)
5 True   6 True   7 True   8 True

Listening Part 1

1 True
2 False. You will hear eight different texts.
3 True   4 True
5 False. The information you hear may be in a different order from the options.
6 False. The words in the options may not be the same as the words you hear.
7 True   8 True

Listening Part 2

1 presentation	5 order
2 minutes	6 changes
3 sentences	7 marks
4 phrase	8 answer

Listening Part 3

1 h   2 c   3 f   4 a   5 d   6 g   7 e   8 b

Listening Part 4

1 two	5 may not be
2 seven	6 no pause
3 three	7 may
4 follow	8 one

Speaking Part 1

1 conversation
2 interview
3 life
4 live
5 information
6 reasons
7 partner
8 minutes

Speaking Part 2

1 True
2 True
3 False. You have to talk about the photographs on your own.
4 True   5 True   6 True
7 False. Your partner will answer a question about your photos after you have spoken for a minute.
8 True

Speaking Part 3/4

1 h   2 f   3 a   4 g   5 d   6 b   7 e   8 c

ACKNOWLEDGEMENTS

The authors and publishers acknowledge the following sources of copyright material and are grateful for the permissions granted. While every effort has been made, it has not always been possible to identify the sources of all the material used, or to trace all copyright holders. If any omissions are brought to our notice, we will be happy to include the appropriate acknowledgements on reprinting and in the next update to the digital edition, as applicable.

Key: TL = Top Left, TR= Top Right, CL = Centre Left, CR = Centre Right, BR = Below Right.

p. 13: pixdeluxe/E+/Getty Images; p. 15: snedorez/iStock/Getty Images; p. 17: Photo and Co/ Photographer's Choice/Getty Images; p. 18: Doug McKinlay/Lonely Planet Images/Getty Images; p. 20: Hill Street Studios/Blend Images/Getty Images; p. 22: Wavebreakmedia Ltd/Getty Images; p. 24: DAVID NUNUK/Science Photo Library/Getty Images; p. 27: Jake Curtis/Iconica/Getty Images; p. 29: Federico Cabrera/LatinContent/Getty Images; p. 30: sbostock/iStock Editorial/Getty Images; p. 32: Toby Burrows/DigitalVision/Getty Images; p. 34: Dreet Production/MITO images/Getty Images; p. 36: ML Harris/Photographer's Choice/Getty Images; p. 38: Javier Pierini/Taxi/Getty Images; p. 40: Justin Lewis/The Image Bank/Getty Images; p. 42: Tom Martin/AWL Images/Getty Images; p. 44: PIERRE VERDY/Staff/AFP/Getty Images; p. 46: monkeybusinessimages/iStock/Getty Images; p. 48: Chung Sung-Jun/Staff/Getty Images; p. 52: Cultura Exclusive/Tim E White/Getty Images; p. 54: Vesna Andjic/ E+/Getty Images; p. 56: Tadeusz Wejkszo/iStock/Getty Images; p. 61: George Wright/Perspectives/ Getty Images; p. 62: Alexandro Auler/STR/LatinContent WO/Getty Images; p. 64: gradyreese/E+/Getty Images; p. 66: EvrenKalinbacak/iStock Editorial/Getty Images; p. 69: PeopleImages.com/DigitalVision/ Getty Images; p. 70: Dave and Les Jacobs/Blend Images/Getty Images; p. 72: Caiaimage/Chris Ryan/ OJO+/Getty Images; p. 74: annedde/E+/Getty Images; p. 76: Jordan Siemens/Iconica/Getty Images; p. 78: Mint Images - Tim Robbins/Getty Images; p. 80: Ezra Bailey/Taxi/Getty Images; p. 83: Tim Melling/Moment/Getty Images; p. 84: Zero Creatives/Cultura/Getty Images; p. 86: James Ross/ Photographer's Choice/Getty Images; p. 89: stevecoleimages/E+/Getty Images; p. 90: Asia Images/ Getty Images; p. 92: FabioFilzi/E+/Getty Images; p. 95: tomazl/E+/Getty Images; p. 96: Tadej Zupancic/iStock/Getty Images; p. 98: Andrew Watson/AWL Images/Getty Images; p. 100: Christopher Futcher/E+/Getty Images; p. 102 (TL): Marcelo Santos/Stone/Getty Images; p. 102 (TR): by Tatsiana Volskaya/Moment/Getty Images; p. 103 (photo 1): anyaberkut/iStock/Getty Images; p. 103 (photo 2): George Clerk/iStock/Getty Images; p. 103 (photo 3): Jupiterimages/Photolibrary/Getty Images; p. 103 (photo 4): Robert Nicholas/OJO Images/Getty Images; p. 104 (CL): Klaus Vedfelt/Taxi/ Getty Images; p. 104 (CR): Tom Werner/Taxi/Getty Images; p. 105 (photo 1): Paul Kennedy/Lonely Planet Images/Getty Images; p. 105 (photo 2): Steve Woods Photography/Cultura/Getty Images; p. 105 (photo 3): PhotoPlus Magazine/Future/Getty Images; p. 105 (photo 4): Maxim Chuvashov/Blend Images/Getty Images; p. 106 (BR): Hill Creek Pictures/UpperCut Images/Getty Images; p. 106 (TL): Berc/iStock/Getty Images; p. 106 (TR): Digital Vision/Photodisc/Getty Images; p. 107 (photo 1): Hero Images/Getty Images; p. 107 (photo 2): Purestock/Getty Images; p. 107 (photo 3): Cultura RM Exclusive/Seb Oliver/Getty Images; p. 107 (photo 4): Westend61/Getty Images; p. 108: Ivanko_ Brnjakovic/iStock/Getty Images; p. 110: Hero Images/Getty Images; p. 112: Digital Vision/Getty Images.

The publishers are grateful to the following contributors:
layout by Q2A Media Services Pvt. Ltd.; audio production by Hart McLeod, Cambridge